DISCOVERING THE RIGVEDA

DISCOVERING THE RIGVEDA

G.N.S. RAGHAVAN

KALPAZ

Discovering the Rigveda

Rs. 540

ISBN: 978-81-7835-778-2

Published in 2009 in India by
Kalpaz Publications
C-30, Satyawati Nagar,
Delhi-110052
E-mail: kalpaz@hotmail.com
Phone : 9212729499

Laser Type Setting by: Rudra Computer Graphics, Delhi

Printed at : Singhal Print Media , Delhi

Contents

Foreword

Sri S.V. Seshadri

The historical evolution of the human fraternity through the stages of community, society and polity is governed at each stage by humanitarian, authoritarian and equalitarian spirit respectively. The early Indian society of the Vedic period was inspired by relations between its members which can be assessed as personal and humane. In the social relationships of the succeeding period, the guiding spirit was mostly functional and possessive. In the present stage of political organization of the society, the relationships are invariably opportunistic and exploitative. These successive changes in the human relationships inevitably had different goals – harmony in the first, acquisitiveness in the second and competitiveness in the last. That the Indian people have stuck to their ideals of a 'caring and sharing' society envisaged by the Rigveda through all these vicissitudes is due to the fact that in all the phases of its history, India has clung steadily to the core values of human relationship, namely peace, order and progress.

Shri. G.N.S. Raghavan has traced the evolution of the successive stages of Indian society during the early, medieval and modern periods in broad sweeps, but with an eye to the essential equations, personal, social and political, that came into play in the changing circumstances. His thesis brings out the fact that while there were problems during each period, there were also influences that mitigated them. He thus takes us through the Charvaka, Buddhist and Jain influences in the earlier stages, the inclusiveness of the bhakti movement and the universalism of Akbar's' Din Ilahi' in the middle period and the nationalism of the independence struggle as ballasts that served the ship of India from any suicidal tilt.

Through the writing of this, Shri. Raghavan has brought his scholarship in literature, experience as a journalist, multi-pointed attention as an administrator and creative curiosity as a thinker to a constructive blend of authorship which speaks for itself in each page. In a sense, he has summarized here the absorptive attitude of the 'argumentative Indian' of Shri. Amartya Sen.

Sri S.V. Seshadri is a very close friend of the author. Both studied together at the Presidency College, Madras. They also worked together in the I&B Ministry, New Delhi.

Preface: Our Unknown *adi kavya*

A major scandal in the world's literary history is the way the Rigveda, India's *adi kavya* or first poetical work (the Ramayana came much later) has been kept outside the ken of most Indians for millennia.

Composed over a period of some three centuries, the poems of the Rigveda expressed the aspiration of the Aryan tribes forming the Rigvedic community for a caring and sharing society, united for self-defence. This humane ethos was supplanted around 1200 Before Common Era (formerly 'Before Christ') by Brahminism, a polar opposite. There were women among the poets of the Rigveda; women as well as Sudras came to be barred from learning or hearing the Vedas. The Rigvedic rishis commended generous help to the needy; Brahminism defined liberality as making gifts to Brahmins.

Recent research has revealed that the Rigveda as it has come down to us with a thousand-odd poems grouped in ten *mandalas* (cycles of poems, or Books) consists of a core composed in the families of six rishis (Books II to VII) while the multi-author Books include matter expressing beliefs and attitudes at variance with egalitarian and comradely values. In *The Vedic People: their history and geography* (Orient Longman, 2000), Rajesh Kochhar indicates the location, but does not examine the nature, of what he calls the old matter and the new matter. The editors of the Sahitya Akademi's *Anthology of Ancient Indian Literature* (2000) stress the 'late' character of the Purusha Sukta but do not suspect that it might be an imposture.

The content analysis undertaken by me and presented in this study shows that the additional matter is Brahminist and has little in common with the pristine, untampered Rigveda. The most audacious insertion is the Purusha Sukta (poem 90, Book X) which proclaims Brahmin supremacy and Sudra servitude as divinely ordained. The other interpolations exhibit the trade marks of Brahminism: hope of an after-life (*svarga* or heaven), belief in *atman* as an entity separate from and surviving the body to take rebirth in accordance with its karma (which has, over the centuries, bred fatalism among individuals and social stagnation); rites and rituals to be performed every day and through the year; and commendation of animal sacrifice.

The leaders of Brahminism discountenanced the writing down of the Vedas even after the advent of writing in the Devanagari script around the 7th century BCE. This was due to the irrational belief that there is spiritual or magical potency in the sound of the *mantras* (verses) chanted with the three *swaras* (accents) of Vedic

Sanskrit as taught by the teacher, a potency which will be lost if the text is read. Even after Vedic Sanskrit became obsolete and unintelligible the Vedas continued to be memorised through mnemonic devices. To this day, what is taught in Veda *pathasalas* is mumbo-jumbo, sound without sense.

But for Sayanacharya (1315–87) the Rigveda which had been in a state of coma might have died for all practical purposes. Sayana wrote a monumental commentary, which was a virtual translation, providing the meaning of every word, phrase and verse as well as his interpretation of the mythological references. He accomplished this feat by drawing on Panini's grammar (3rd century BCE) of Vedic and classical Sanskrit, Yaska's Nirukta (Vedic etymology) of the 6th century BCE; and numerous Nighantus (books of synonyms). With the Rigveda thus made intelligible, the fraternity of Sanskrit scholars could have spread knowledge of it through translations and condensed accounts in Sanskrit as well as the spoken languages of the people. The Rigveda could have become, like the two epics, part of popular culture. But that did not happen, because of the paralysing faith in the sound of the Vedas. What our Sanskritists failed to do was done eventually by Max Muller and other Western scholars who revealed the meaning of the Vedas to the English-knowing in India and throughout the world.

What is presented here is not a statistically representative sample of the subjects addressed in the hymns of the Rigveda. Repetitive praise of divinities like Agni, Indra and the Soma drink occupy a large proportion of the work; only some examples are reproduced. Attention is focussed instead on the most precious features of the Rigveda, which even perceptive Western scholars have not noticed adequately: the ethical orientation which was to find resonance in post-Sangam Tamil poetry; insight into the working of the human mind and motivation, as in the poem on the losing gambler which anticipates Vyasa's Yudhishtira and Dostoevsky's tragic hero; bold confronting of a subject as challenging as incest; existential introspection ('What thing I truly am, I know not'); and the speculation by the Rigvedic sages, who were the world's earliest free-thinkers, on the possible but not necessary existence of a Creator God.

Such passages, attractive to contemporary sensibility, make the Rigveda, more than 3000 years old, perennially modern and therefore richly deserving of description as a classic. In addition to presenting the memorable features of the untampered Rigveda, I have surveyed the ritual-ridden and casteist (not to say racist) Brahminism which supplanted the Rigvedic ethos. I discuss also the subsequent softening and humanising of Brahminism by reforming influences: the nobler Upanishads; the rationalist Charvaka thinkers; the compassionate teaching of Mahavira and Buddha; the texts on Dharma and the epics which, though mainly Brahminist in tenor, include passages with a humanist import; and the Bhakti movement. These turned Brahminism into the popular Hinduism which has endured to this day.

I shall feel rewarded if this study stimulates some readers to undertake their own exploration of the universe of the Vedas, and to relish and share with others what they find attractive and intellectually stimulating. Immediately, scholars versed in a widely spoken Indian language besides English can render service of inestimable value by translating and publishing all or many of the poems presented in this volume, along with related information. It will reveal the Rigveda as the Gangotri of India's religion and philosophy.

If the generality of our Brahminists and Sanskritists should feel mortified that they have not been able to keep the Rigveda firmly under lock for longer than three millennia, it will serve them right. More important, it will help to correct an ancient intellectual and moral wrong perpetrated by those who appointed themselves as the sole custodians of learning.

Chennai **G.N.S. Raghavan**

April 2007

1

A Worldly People with Humane Ethics

Why is the Rigveda, of the second millennium Before Common Era (formerly 'Before Christ') regarded as the starting point of India's cultural history rather than the well-developed urban civilisation of the Indus Valley which flourished earlier?

The remains of the Indus civilisation were discovered by accident in 1856, during British rule, when a railway line was being laid from Karachi to Lahore. John Brunton, who was among those engaged in this work, came across huge dusty mounds under which burnt bricks were found. "I had been much exercised in my mind", he writes in his memoirs, "How we were to get ballast. If all I heard were true, this ruined city, built of bricks, would form a grand quarry."

Enigma of Harappa

In delayed follow-up of this discovery, archaeologists led by Sir John Marshall and his Indian colleague R. D. Banerji uncovered in 1923 an ancient civilisation that has come to be named after the Indus Valley. Among the principal sites were Harappa (West Punjab), Kalibanga (Rajasthan), Mohenjodaro (Sind) and a dockyard at Lothal (Gujarat). In his book on 'Mohenjodaro and the Indus Civilisation', Marshall refers to the excellent town planning and drainage system, granaries, and public baths of the Indus cities and draws an interesting contrast with other ancient civilisations: "There is nothing that we know of in prehistoric Egypt or Mesopotamia or anywhere in western Asia to compare with the well-built baths and commodious houses of the citizens of Mohenjodaro. In those countries much money and thought were lavished on the building of magnificent temples for the gods and palaces and tombs of kings, but the rest of the people seemingly had to content themselves with insignificant dwellings of mud. In the Indus Valley the picture is reversed, and the finest structures are those erected for the convenience of citizens."

In contrast to the abundant archaeological evidence of the Harappan civilisation, there is no literary evidence. The script of samples of writing that have been found on some seals has not yet been decisively deciphered. The world-view or religion of the Harappan people can only be guessed at from artefacts like the seals depicting a humped bull, phallic symbols, and figurines. There is no connection between them and the natural forces personified as divinities in the cosmic religion of the Rigvedic Aryans.

Were the Harappans Dravidians, or were they Sumerians? The historian R.C. Majumdar says: "Some believe that these two were identical. There is also a theory that the Indus people were Aryans, but this at present finds few supporters. And there is always the possibility that the people of the Indus Valley might have belonged to an altogether separate race." (*An Advanced History of India*, Macmillan, 1950, p. 23)

As we shall see, there developed many differences, several of them for the worse, between the beliefs and practices of the Rigvedic period and the Brahminism which supplanted the Rigvedic ethos by about 1200 BCE. (I employ the Anglicised spelling Brahmin rather than Brahman – pronounced Brahman – to denote the caste. This is in order to strip the caste name of pretensions to proximity if not identity with Brahman, the All. And the term is used by me to denote a Brahmin supremacist, who is usually also a male chauvinist.) Though there were women among the poet-thinkers who wrote the Rigvedic verses, Brahminists denied access to learning both to women and Sudras. And while the Rigvedic poets defined generosity as gifts to the needy, Brahminists defined it as gifts to Brahmins. However, there are several aspects in which there is a significant continuity between the Rigvedic way of life and the gradually reformed Brahminism that prevails now as Hinduism. One is worship of the Sun as in the following Gayatri verse from hymn 62 of Book III of the Rigveda.

We meditate upon that adorable effulgence of the resplendent vivifier, Savitar;

May he stimulate our intellects.

Another is the invocation of the Fire God as witness of all sacraments including marriage. A third is the worship of feminine deities, unknown to Christianity and Islam, such as Ushas the Dawn goddess and Bhoodevi the Earth goddess.

In the circumstances, there is no alternative to regarding the Rigveda as the starting point of the chequered course of India's religion and philosophy spanning more than 3500 years. There could not have been a more impressive beginning.

The Rigveda is a grand testament of natural religion, the name given in recent years by Western writers to the beliefs and values of people in different parts of the world before the birth of Christianity. Formerly Christian writers employed offensive terms like heathen, barbarian and pagan for those who did not profess Judaism or Christianity. Islam too was held in contempt as heathen till it proved its might in the Crusades. It was then classed along with Judaism and Christianity as religions which were, as the *Concise Oxford Dictionary* puts it, 'revealed by inspiration or supernatural means'. The term natural religion as applied to non-Semitic faiths is not offensive. On the contrary, it suggests freedom from superstitious belief in prophets, or a son, sent by God which is at the heart of revealed religions. An alternative description is 'primordial religiousness'. This felicitous expression has been coined by Raimundo Panikkar, professor of religious studies at the University of California, Santa Barbara. It avoids the association of 'religion' with theology and superstition; and the word 'primordial' (from the beginning) avoids the pretentiousness of sanatana (eternal, without beginning) as in sanatana dharma. The *COD* speaks of natural religion as 'instinctive, based on the innate moral sense', and of natural theology as 'knowledge of god as gained by reason and light of nature'. Though the *COD* is grounded in Christianity which came much later, these hints are useful for understanding the Rigvedic ethos.

The Four Vedas

Before proceeding to present the world-view and ethical philosophy of the Rigveda (from rik – verse, and vid – to know) let me briefly survey the chronology and the nature of contents of the four Vedas. The Rigveda, which is the primary Veda, is believed to have been composed between 1500 and 1200 BCE. It is the longest, and contains a thousand odd poems of exalted thought and expression with upwards of 10,000 stanzas. These 'knowledge verses' are grouped in ten mandalas or Books (cycles of poems). Six of them, Books II to VII, were each composed by a rishi — reacher (after knowledge), or seer – and by his sons and pupils in the family. The rishis were: Gritsamada, Visvamitra, Vamadeva, Atri, Bharadvaja and Vasishta. The poems in the other Books are by more than one author, and they include women poets. Book IX brings together all the poems in praise of Soma, the exhilarating drink of which both the Rigvedic gods and men were fond, and which was offered as an oblation in the sacrificial fire.

Though the hymns of the Rigveda address and eulogise various divinities, they really express the poets' astonished delight in the workings of nature. They cherish the dawn (Ushas) which heralds each new day of life, express wonder and awe at lightning and thunder (Indra); and revel in the rain (Parjanya) that nourishes life on earth.

Many of the poems – though all are referred to as 'hymns' – are on non-religious themes. In several poems there is no apparent connection between certain verses; they may have got transposed from one hymn to another. Not all stanzas of a hymn are addressed necessarily to the deity or other subject of the poem. A stanza may be spoken by one character, and the next by another, as in the Yama–Yami dialogue. In a Brahminist poem describing a horse sacrifice, the poet alternately addresses the victim and its slayers. But the identity of the speaker and of the person addressed can be inferred from the context. There is naturally repetition and monotony in Book IX devoted exclusively to poems by different authors in praise of Soma. There is also repetition elsewhere, in the hymns in praise of Indra, Agni and other leading divinities, since each of the six rishis wrote several poems in their praise. It will be enough for the general reader to sample them. Similarly of little interest to the general reader today are the references in the poems to ancient mythology. Foreign scholars have expended much labour on trying to clarify these references, and their work is commendable. But, with the exception of Max Muller, foreign scholars have failed to appreciate the grandeur of thought in many of the poems and the non-theistic but deeply ethical orientation of the natural religion of the Rigveda.

Of the other Vedas, the Atharva – the second longest, with some 6000 stanzas – has some poems that are close to the spirit of the Rigveda in the celebration of the awesome mystery of creation. They had perhaps begun to be composed at about the same time as the Rigveda, though recognition of the Atharva as a Veda came very late. This was because the critics did not approve of the presence in the Atharvaveda of a large number of poems which are in the nature of charms against disease or against a co-wife or other rival to a man's affections, and of imprecations and curses. These are expressions of the popular culture of the time. M. N. Dutt's English translation (Parimal Publications, Delhi, 1906, reprint 1986) includes the following:

This woman shall be subjected to thee,
O king Yama, (till then) let her be fixed
To the house of her mother, or her brother,
or her father.
Another woman exclaims:
As the best of the plants thou art
reputed, O herb,
Turn this man for me today into a
eunuch that wears his hair dressed.

In the light of its uneven quality, the Atharvaveda is regarded as a Veda-by-courtesy.

The Samaveda has some 2000 stanzas, most of them taken from the Rigveda. It is significant only as an aid to the singing of Vedic verses, whose language carries three swaras (accents).

The Yajurveda has prose as well as verse units, numbering about 2000. It is classed as a sacrificial text, distinguished from recited hymns and chants. All these three subsidiary Vedas are believed to have been composed over two centuries from 1200 to 1000 BCE and even later. The deterioration in values which set in during the post-Rigvedic period can be seen in the Brahminists rites, ritual and superstition found in the Yajurveda.

The caste system had become settled by the time of the Yajurveda. In a historical survey of the Vedic period, C. G. Kashihar writes in Vol. I of *Ancient Indian Literature: An Anthology* (Sahitya Akademi, 2000): "The chronological difference between the composition of the Rigvedic hymns and those of the Yajurveda is marked by a significant development in the religion and philosophy of the ancient Indians, and also by changes in social conditions .... Society had settled down in the Punjab and other northern parts of India up to the confluence of the Ganga and the Yamuna in the east. Men who belonged to the first three social orders were entitled to study the Veda (collective singular) and practise sacrificial religion. Even though elaborate rituals were developed under magical influence, ethical values were honoured. The aim of life was to attain heaven (*svarga*) after death by performing sacrifices as prescribed." In contrast, the Rigvedic people were this-worldly, and had no notion of an after-life.

Another belief which grew with the ascendancy of Brahminism was in ritual purity and ritual impurity. How impure a woman was deemed to be during the menstrual period is seen from the following account, in a prose unit of the Yajurveda, of how Indra got rid of a part of the guilt of slaying a Brahmin:

"He appealed to a concourse of women, 'Take the third of my guilt'. They said: 'Let us choose a boon; let us obtain offspring from after the menses; let us enjoy intercourse at will up to birth'. They took a third of his guilt. It became a woman with stained garments. Therefore one should not converse with a woman with stained garments; one should not sit with her, nor eat her food. The son born of intercourse with a woman with stained garments is accursed. The son born of a woman bathing in her menses period is fated to drown; the son born of one who cuts her nails has bad nails; the son born of one who drinks from a leaf is drunken; the son of one who drinks from a mutilated vessel is mutilated. For three nights she should keep a vow and should drink from her hand, or from a perfect vessel, to guard her offspring."

Every Hindu family of the first three castes belongs to a Gotra, named after the progenitor traced back through the male line. It also professes one or other of the four Vedas. The one to which most families belong is the Yajurveda, doubtless because it was studied by the Brahmin priests who conducted the rituals prescribed in it. The rituals observed now-a-days are mostly domestic and connected with rites of passage from life to death. These domestic rites are got performed by Brahmin priests in the homes of many Sudras (who are merely 'once-born').

The continuing hold of Yajurvedic-Brahminist beliefs regarding ritual impurity is illustrated by the recent controversy over the employment of women as barbers at the holy Tirupati shrine in Andhra Pradesh. Many men and women pilgrims get their heads tonsured on a visit to Tirupati. Following a request from some women pilgrims that they would like to be spared the lustful looks and touches of some of the male barbers, the Tirumala Tirupati Devasthanam board decided in April 2005 to recruit about a hundred women barbers. There were protests from the heads of some religious sects, and from male barbers. Following this, and after consulting those versed in the post-Rigvedic texts known as Agamas dealing with temple architecture and worship, the TTD board at a meeting on 21st May 2005 dropped the plan to recruit women barbers. In another turn, following protests from women's organisations, the TTD in July 2006 initiated the process of recruiting women as barbers.

As will be examined more fully in the third chapter, Brahminist beliefs and values were injected into the Rigveda itself in the form of interpolations. The most audacious of these is the proclamation in poem 90 of Book X, known as the Purusha Sukta, of Brahmin supremacy and Sudra servitude as divinely ordained. This new matter which is foreign to the spirit of the untampered Rigveda was probably added while the Atharva, Sama and Yajur Vedas were being composed. What I proceed to present regarding the world-view and values of the Rigvedic rishis is from the untampered, pristine portions which fortunately constitute the bulk of the Rigveda as it has come down to us. Mercifully it is easy to separate the Rigvedic grain from the chaff because the newly added matter identifies itself by its Brahminist content.

Naturalistic and Ethical Divinities

Moved by the beauty and mystery of creation, the Rigvedic rishis composed hymns celebrating nature and the cosmos. Natural forces were to them divinities. In addition even the man-made Soma drink was accorded the status of a divinity and eulogised, along with Indra, warrior-god who was patron and protector of the Rigvedic community of Aryan tribes, and Agni who carried to the gods the oblations offered in the sacrificial fire.

Indra is the deity addressed in a fourth of the thousand odd hymns of the Rigveda. A god of the thunderbolt, he vanquishes the demon of drought by releasing the waters, and wins light by overcoming darkness. At the same time he is the favourite national god of the Rigvedic people and helps them defeat their enemies. Awe and supplication are prominent in the hymns addressed to him. Given below are some verses from poem 12 in Book II, given in prose translation in A Vedic Reader by A. A. Macdonell (published in England, 1917; Indian reprint, Motilal Banarsidass, 1992):

Greatness of Indra

Who made firm the quaking earth, who set at rest the agitated mountains; who measured out the air more widely, who supported heaven: he, O men, is Indra.

Who having slain the serpent released the seven streams, who drove out the cows by the unclosing of Vala, who between two rocks produced fire, victor in battles: he, O men, is Indra.

Without whom men do not conquer, whom they when fighting call on for help; who has been a match for everyone, who moves the immovable, he O men, is Indra.

Who with his aid helps him that presses Soma, him that bakes, him that offers praise, him that has prepared the sacrifice; whom prayer, whom Soma, whom this gift strengthens; he, O men, is Indra.

The chief wise god who as soon as born surpassed the gods in power; before whose vehemence the two worlds trembled by reason of the greatness of his valour: he, O men, is Indra.

Agni is addressed in 200 and more hymns, next only to Indra. Macdonell says about the mythology of Agni: "From the dry sticks Agni is born living; as soon as born the child devours his parents. Being produced every morning, he is young. At the same time no sacrifice is older than Agni, for he conducted the first sacrifice." Here are extracts from poem 1, Book I, written after sacrifices came to be performed inside homes as well as in the open.

Agni: Pillar of Fire

I magnify Agni the domestic priest, the divine ministrant of the sacrifice, the invoker, best bestower of treasure.

May Agni, the invoker of wise intelligence, the true, of most brilliant fame, the god, come with the gods.

O Agni be easy of access to us, as a father to his son; abide with us for our well-being.

There are more than 100 hymns to Soma, which celebrate the process of making the drink, right from pressing the stalks for the juice. The plant was gathered by moonlight on certain mountains and was therefore referred to as Indu (moon plant). Here are extracts from a poem on Soma.

Dear to gods and men

Wisely I have partaken of the sweet food that stirs good thoughts, best banisher of care, to which all gods and mortals, calling it honey, come together.

We have drunk Soma; we have become immortal; we have gone to the light; we have found the gods. What can hostility now do to us, and what the malice of mortal man, O immortal one?

Of thee pressed we would partake as of paternal wealth. King Soma, prolong our years as the sun the days of spring.

In the hymns addressed to feminine deities there is joyful adoration as well as grateful affection like that of a child for its mother. Ushas, the goddess of Dawn, is celebrated in many hymns. Here are a half-dozen stanzas from poem 51 of Book IV.

Hymn to Ushas

Forth from the darkness, in the region eastward, this most abundant splendid light hath mounted.

Now verily the far-refulgent Mornings, Daughters of Heaven, bring welfare to the people.

The richly coloured Dawns have mounted eastward, like pillars mounted at our sacrifices;

And flushing far, splendid and purifying, unbarred the portals of the fold of darkness,

With horses harnessed by eternal Order, Goddesses, swiftly round the worlds ye travel,

Arousing from their rest, O Dawns, the sleeping, all that lives, man, bird and beast, to motion.

Thus they go forth with undiminished colours, these Mornings similar, in self-same fashion.

Concealing the gigantic might of darkness with radiant bodies bright and pure and shining.

O Goddesses, O Heaven's refulgent Daughters, bestow upon us wealth with store of children.

As from our pleasant place of rest ye rouse us, may we be masters of heroic vigour.

Well skilled in lore of sacrifice, ye Daughters of Heaven, refulgent Dawns, I thus address you:

May we be glorious among the people. May Heaven vouehsafe us this, and Earth the Goddess.

As remarked earlier, portions of the Atharvaveda are similar to the Rigveda in poetic quality and thought content. A selection from the 63 verses of a hymn to mother earth from the Atharvaveda are reproduced here. They might as well be from the Rigveda.

Paean to Mother Earth

The earth that has height, and slopes, and Great Plains, that supports the plants of manifold virtue, free from the pressure that comes from the midst of men, shall spread out for us, and fit herself for us!

The earth upon which the attendant waters jointly flow by day and night unceasingly, shall pour out milk for us in rich streams and, moreover, sprinkle us with glory!

Him that hates us, O earth, him that battles against us, him that is hostile towards us with his mind and with his weapons, do you subject to us, anticipating (our wish) by deed!

Agni is in the earth, in the plants, the waters hold Agni. Agni is in the stones, Agni is within men, Agnis are within cattle, within horses. Agni glows from the sky; to Agni, the god, belongs the broad air. The mortals kindle Agni, the bearer of oblation, that loves ghee.

That fragrance of yours which has entered into the lotus, that fragrance, O earth, the immortals of yore gathered up at the marriage of Surya, with that make me fragrant.

That fragrance of yours which is in men, the loveliness and charm that is male and female, that which is in steeds and heroes, that which is in the wild animals with trunks, the lustre that is in the maiden, O earth, with that do you blend us !

As long as I look upon thee, O earth, with Surya (the sun) as my companion, so long shall my sight not fail, as year followeth upon year !

When, as I lie, I turn upon my right or left side, O earth, when stretched out we lie with our ribs upon thee pressing, do not, O earth that lieth close to everything, there injure us! What, O earth, I dig out of thee, quickly shall that grow again; may. I not, O pure one, pierce thy vital spot, not thy heart!

The earth upon whom the noisy mortals sing and dance, upon whom they fight, upon whom resounds the roaring drum, shall drive forth our enemies, shall make us free from rivals!

The earth that holds people of manifold varied speech, of different customs according to their habitations, as a reliable milch-cow that does not kick, shall she milk for me a thousand streams of wealth.

The serpent, the scorpion with thirsty fangs, that hibernating torpidly lies upon thee, the worm and whatever living thing, O earth, that moves in the rainy season, shall, when it creeps, not creep upon us; with what is auspicious be gracious to us.

The earth holds the fool and holds the wise, endures that good and bad dwell (upon her).

The earth upon whom the biped birds fly together, the flamingoes, eagles, birds of prey, and fowls; upon whom Matarisvan the wind hastens, raising the dust and tossing the trees, the earth upon whom day and night jointly, black and bright, have been decreed, the broad earth covered and enveloped with rain, shall kindly place us into every pleasant abode!

O mother earth, kindly set me down upon a well-founded place! With (father) heaven co-operating, O wise one, place me into happiness and prosperity!

Honoured Place for Women

An honoured place for woman in the home and in society was the counterpart of the worship of feminine deities. Girls received education (which at that time mainly meant learning the Vedas) along with boys. Both were invested with the sacred thread, marking initiation into studies, at a ceremony known as Upanayanam. Raj Bali Pandey, former professor of Ancient Indian History and Culture at the Banaras Hindu University, says in *Hindu Samskaras: a socio-religious study of the Hindu sacraments* (Vikrama Publications, Banaras) that there was a decline in the age of marriage of girls due to “the stoppage of Vedic study and the Upanayanam of girls.” He cites as another reason for the institution of pre-puberty marriages the insecurity of social life following the foreign invasions of India from the 3rd century BCE. With national revival and social stabilisation in the Gupta period there was a revival of adult marriages which continued till the Muslim invasions.

To reinforce the custom of early marriage, myths were invented to the effect that a girl’s physical and mental growth were presided over by Soma, lord of the vegetable world; by Gandharva, master of the graces; and by Agni, the lord of fire who brings about the menstrual flow "and then gives her to man, her fourth *pati* or lord." Over time, "Soma, Gandharva and Agni who were believed to help the physical development of a girl came to be held as enjoyers of her person. Hence the anxiety to give her away in marriage"

Poem 85 in Book X of the Rigveda is a marriage hymn – an obvious interpolation – which presents both the Rigvedic ethos of freedom and vigour. Following are excerpts from the poem:

Marriage Hymn

O Gandharva, get away from here,
we pray to you with homage.
Look for another one who is still to be married,
leave this bride with her husband.
Some obtained the bride first,
and Gandharva obtained her next,
Agni was your third husband,
and one born among men is your fourth.
May Soma give her to Gandharva,
may Gandharva give her to Agni,
Agni has just given her
to me with wealth and sons.
O bountiful Indra, make this bride
the mother of good sons,
of good fortune. Put in her ten sons,
make the husband the eleventh.
O bride, manage like a queen
in the house of your father and mother in law,
Reign like a delightful queen
over your husband's sister and brothers.

May the universal gods
blend our hearts together,
may the waters unite them.

Several women distinguished themselves in the wider world beyond the home. A.C. Bose formerly of Delhi University, versed both in English and Sanskrit, names women rishis (sages) who wrote some of the Rigvedic poems: Ghosha, the daughter of King Kakshivan, Vak, said to be the daughter of the rishi Ambhirina, Apala, Indrani, Sachi Paulomi, and Yami. (*Seers and Thinkers* in the Cultural Leaders of India series, Publications Division, 1979). Some scholars add the names of Visvavara, of the family of Atri, and Lopamudra, wife of the sage Agastya.

Here are some lines from a hymn addressed by Ghosha to the Asvins, the twin heralds of the dawn:

Asvins

Your radiant Chariot – whither goes it on its way? Who decks it for you, Heroes, for its happy course starting at daybreak, visiting each morning every house, borne hitherward through prayer unto the sacrifice?

Where are you, Asvins, in the evening, where at morn? Where is your halting place, where rest ye for the night? O Heroes, this I beg of you. 'Be near me in the day, be near me in the night'.

Poem 125 in Book X celebrates Vak. It is, says Griffith, "Speech personified, the Word, the first creation and representative of Spirit, and the means of communication between men and gods." (*The Hymns of the Rigveda* translated by Ralph T. H. Griffith, second edition 1896, Indian reprint Motilal Banarsidass). The author identifies herself with the subject of the poem, and declares spiritedly:

Vak

I travel with the Rudras and the Vasus, with the Adityas and the All-Gods I wander.

I hold aloft both Varuna and Mitra, Indra and Agni, and the Pair of Asvins.

I cherish and sustain high-swelling Soma; and Tvastar, I support Pusan and Bhaga.

I load with wealth the zealous sacrificer who pours the juice and offers his oblation.

I am the Queen, the gatherer-up of treasures, most thoughtful first of those who merit worship. Thus gods have established me in many places with many homes to enter and abide in.

Each man who sees, breathes, hears the word outspoken

They know it not, but yet they dwell beside me. Hear, one and all, the truth as I declare it.

I verily, myself announce and utter the word that gods and men alike shall welcome.

I make the man I love exceeding mighty, make him a sage, a rishi, a Brahman.

I bend the bow for Rudra that his arrow may strike and slay the hater of devotion.

I rouse and order battle for the people, and I have penetrated Earth and Heaven.

On the world's summit I bring forth the Father; my home is in the water, in the ocean.

Thence I extend over all existing creatures, and touch even yonder heaven with my forehead.

I breathe a strong breath like the wind and tempest, the while I hold together all existence.

Beyond this wide earth and beyond the heavens I have become mighty in my grandeur.

Ascribed to another woman poet, Visvavara, is a hymn to Agni (Book V, 28) from which some lines are reproduced below:

> Agni inflamed hath sent to heaven his lustre;
> he shines forth widely, turning into Morning.
> Eastward the ladle goes that brings all blessing,
> praising the gods with homage and oblation.
> Enkindled, thou art King of the immortal world;
> him who brings offerings thou attendest for his weal.
> Thy glory, Agni, I adore; exalted in thy strength,
> A Steer of brilliant splendour, thou art lighted
> well at sacred rites.
> Agni, invoked and kindled, serve the gods, thou
> skilled in sacrifice:
> For thou art bearer of our gifts.

Poem 179 in Book X addressed to Rati or Love, deals frankly with Lopamudra's desire to be caressed by her aged husband Agastya. The poem concludes with the lines:

Agastya thus, toiling with strong endeavour, wishing for children, progeny and power.

Cherished – a sage of mighty strength – both classes, and with the gods obtained his prayer's fulfilment.

(Griffith says that 'both classes' probably refers to the priests and to the princes or other wealthy institutors of sacrifices.)

FOR A CARING AND COHESIVE SOCIETY

The Rigvedic people were open to supranatural or mystical experience, but were not superstitious. They had no notion of an atman (soul) independent of the body and surviving it to take rebirth in an endless cycle of karma-determined existence, which was to become a central dogma of Hinduism. They prayed for a full 100 - year span of life, and the only immortality they looked forward to was through the genes. A hymn to Rudra (poem 33, Book II) prays:

May we, O Rudra, be born again
through our progeny.
May I attain, O Rudra, a hundred winters.

The sages commended through their poems the values that people should cultivate in order to live in freedom and well-being, in this world and in this one life, as inter-dependent members of a caring and sharing society. This was regarded as necessary for social health and strength. To this end, some of the divinities lauded in the hymns were spoken of as guardians of this or that social virtue. Thus Mitra was hailed as the god of contract, or keeping troth. Mitra was believed to keep watch on persons who had entered into an agreement. Poem 59 in Book III says:

Mitra : God of Truth

Mitra when invoked
makes men enter into agreements;
Mitra watches men with unblinking eyes.
Offer an oblation with ghee to Mitra.
May that mortal enjoy sustenance
who, O son of Aditi, strives to keep the vow.
He who is aided by you is not slain,
or conquered; vice afflicts him
neither from near nor from afar.

R. N. Dandekar in *Sources of Indian Tradition* (Columbia University Press, 1963, Indian reprint Motilal Banarsidass) says while introducing poem 85 in Book V of the Rigveda : "Varuna is the administrator of the cosmic law (*rta*, dharma) which regulates all activities in this world. He pours out the rain but sees to it that one ocean is not filled to overflowing by many rivers. This upholder of cosmic order is also regarded as the lord of human morality. It is the function of Varuna to ensure that there occurs no transgression of the law, cosmic or human." Extracts from a prose translation follow.

Varuna: Order, Cosmic and Moral

Varuna has extended the air above the trees, he has put strength in horses, milk in cows, will power in hearts, fire in waters, the sun in the heaven, and Soma upon the mountain.

Varuna poured out the leather-bag, opening downward, upon the heaven and the earth and the mid-region. Thereby does the lord of the whole creation moisten thoroughly the expanse of the earth. No one, indeed, dare impugn this great magic-work of the wisest god, namely that the many glistening streams, pouring forth, do not fill up one ocean with water.

If we Varuna, have offended against a friend, or if we have offended against an all-time comrade or an inmate – whether belonging to us, O Varuna, or a stranger – do you remove that offence from us.

Varuna is also guardian of truth, and on this aspect poem 76 in Book IV of the Atharvaveda (Saunaka recension) says:

Guardian of Truth: Varuna

If a man stands, walks, or sneaks about, if he goes slinking away, if he goes into his hiding place, if two persons sit together and scheme, king Varuna is there as a third, and knows it.

Both this earth here and also yonder broad sky whose boundaries are far away belong to King Varuna. Moreover, these two oceans are the loins of Varuna, yea, he is hidden in this small drop of water.

King Varuna sees through all that is between heaven and earth, and all that is beyond. He has counted the winks of men's eyes. As a winning gamester puts down his dice, thus does he establish these laws.

May all your fateful toils which, seven by seven, three-fold, lie spread out, ensnare him that speaks falsehood; him that speaks the truth they shall let go !

In this apostrophising of ethical values as divinities there is an element of the anthropomorphism which was to become pervasive in popular Hinduism. However, in Rigvedic times no images were made for worship, either at home or in temples. There are, moreover, poems which directly celebrate good qualities. The following verses are from a hymn to liberality (poem 117, Book X):

Liberality

The Gods have not ordained hunger to be our death: even to the well-fed man comes death in varied shape.

The riches of the liberal never waste away, while he who will not give finds none to comfort him.

The man with food in store who, when the needy comes in miserable case begging for bread to eat, hardens his heart against him – even when of old he did him service – finds not one to comfort him.

Bounteous is he who gives unto the beggar who comes to him in want of food, and feeble. Success attends him in the shout of battle. He makes a friend of him in future troubles.

No friend is he who to his friend and comrade who comes imploring food, will offer nothing.

Let him depart – no home is that to rest in – and rather seek a stranger to support him.

Let the rich satisfy the poor implorer, and bend his eye upon a longer pathway.

Riches comes now to one, now to another, and like the wheels of cars are ever rolling.

All guilt is he who eats with no partaker.

T. R. Griffith in his translation of the Rigvedic hymns explains the opening lines of the poem: "Men must not attempt to justify their refusal of food to the hungry by saying that the Gods send hunger as a punishment for sin." This is significant, and is contrary the Karma theory of rebirth in Brahminism which supplanted the Rigvedic religion. In the Katha Upanishad, for example, Yama says to Nachiketa: "I shall tell you how the self fares after death. It transmigrates after death. Some souls enter the womb for acquiring bodies. And others (extremely inferior ones) follow the state of motionless things like trees, in accordance with each one's work in this life." (Translation by Swami Gambhirananda, Advaita Ashrama, Calcutta.)

The poet -sages urged harmony and concord among members of the Rigvedic community. The last hymn (poem 191, Book X) is on this subject. The priest addresses the first stanza to Agni, and the following three stanzas to those assembled at the sacrifice.

Hymn of Concord

O Bull, Agni,
you gather, by and by,
all the riches even of strangers.
Bring to us the riches you possess
May you all go together
may you speak together
may your minds be in accord.
The mantra is common
to those assembled here,
their place of assembly is common;
their mind is common,
their understanding is common;

I recite a common mantra for you,
I offer a common offering.
May your intention be at one,
may your hearts be at one,
may your mind be at one
so that all of you
can form a splendid union.

Unity For Forceful Self-defence

Concord was commended not only for the sake of social harmony, but as a condition necessary for the Rigvedic community to defend itself against those hostile to it. Self-defence was necessary because the Rigvedic people did not inhabit an island of peace surrounded by an ocean of tranquillity. As in other parts of the world at the stage of tribal organisation, the Aryan tribes in the north-west of India had to guard their territory from encroachment by others. These outsiders are often referred to as *dasyus*. Indra and other gods are gratefully praised by the Rigvedic poets for enabling them to defeat the enemies.

Poem 8, Book II, concludes with the lines:
May we with Agni's, Indra's help, with
Soma's, yea, of all the gods,
Uninjured dwell together still, and conquer
those who fight with us.

The hymn to the Earth goddess, cited earlier, prays at more than one place for success against enemies. Poem 33 in Book II addressed to Rudra, who is a god of fierce aspect, pleads:

Oh mighty Rudra, when you are praised,
have mercy for the singer.
Let your missiles strike someone other than us.

A hymn to harmony in the Atharvaveda (IX, 4) says:

May your hearts be common, your minds too! Agni is your common god. United may you serve the country! Collective is your valour. May you protect one another collectively! Hurl the feathered arrow collectively at others!

Book X has two hymns (83 and 84) invoking Manyu (anger), addressed as a deity, to inspire the singer and his people to fight the enemy. Here are some of the verses :

Come hitther Manyu, mightier than the mighty, chase with thy fervour for ally, our foemen. Victorious subduer, vouehsafe to us superior strength in battle.

Approach, and on my right hand, hold thy station; so shall we slay a multitude of foemen.

The best of meath I offer to support thee: may we be first to drink thereof in quiet.

Alone of many thou art worshipped, Manyu; sharpen the spirit of each clan for battle.

That force must be employed to repel an enemy attack is self-evident. But in India after Bhagavan Buddha, Emperor Asoka and Mahatma Gandhi it has become necessary to state the obvious. Asoka renounced war after his conquest of Kalinga and conversion to Buddhism. The death and devastation during the war had made him feel remorseful. He did not have to think about the ethics of a war of self-defence since he had built a very powerful state and there was no challenger in sight. But after Asoka's death it was not long before

India became the victim of attacks from the northwest. The invaders had to face, mainly, Buddhist monasteries rather than fortresses. Gandhi, deeply influenced by Jainism which was prevalent in his native Gujarat, made a fetish of Ahimsa. This is a term which should translate as non-cruelty but has come to be equated with non-violence, non-killing and non-retaliation. His counsel to fellow-Hindus was to 'die without killing' when faced with belligerent Muslims.

This prescription of suicide was first put forward by Gandhi in the course of an article on 'Hindu-Muslim tension: its cause and cure' in *Young India* of 29th May 1924: "There is no doubt in my mind that in the majority of quarrels the Hindus come out second best. My own experience confirms the opinion that the Mussalman as a rule is a bully, and the Hindu as a rule is a coward." But though Gandhi said he preferred violence to cowardice, he did not advise Hindus to fight back. Instead, he wrote: "Those Hindus who ran away to save their lives would have been truly non-violent and would have covered themselves with glory, and added lustre to their faith and won the friendship of their Mussalman assailants if they had stood bare breast with smiles on their lips, and died at their post."

Gandhi remained constant in this view. In 1947, when raiders from Pakistan attacked Jammu-Kashmir, he said he would demonstrate that the state could be saved through non-violent means if he could have a 'hundred thousand volunteers for suicide'.

The proposition that mass suicide is the answer to an enemy attack is laughable. Yet in India during the 20th century Gandhi was revered widely as an apostle of non-violence. In the 21st century, successive governments of different political hue have not retaliated against the continuing killings by Islamist militants in Jammu-Kashmir. Nor against the serial bomb blasts in various cities carried out by Pakistani and Indian saboteurs including illegal Bangladeshi immigrants financed, trained and equipped by Pakistan. The people of Rigvedic times would have found this supineness shocking.

2

World's Earliest Free-thinkers

Free from the theology and dogma of organised religion, the Rigvedic poet-thinkers did not have ready-made answers to questions concerning the origin of the universe or the existence of an extra-cosmic God who created and controls it. Most of them were content to marvel at the life around them on earth and the stars and the moon and the sun above.

Some did think that there might be a designer behind the design, but they could not give any particular form or name to such a possible God. Hymn 121 in Book X is addressed to Ka (Who?), the Unknown God. The tenor of the poem is panthesist, not theist. It addresses an unknown creator god and does not convey the feeling of devotion to a personal god which is characteristic of theism. Given below is V. Raghavan's prose translation of the poem (*The Indian Heritage*, 1958, p.14).

God: Who ?

The creator was born in the beginning; coming into being, he became one Lord of the created; he props up this earth, and this heaven as well. That someone who is God, let us worship with oblation.

Who by His greatness became the sole king of the world that breathes and the world that winks, and who rules over these bipeds and quadrupeds. That someone who is God, let us worship with oblation.

He whose glory the snow-laden mountains are, to whom belongs the sea along with the rivers, whose arms are those quarters, That someone who is God, let us worship with oblation.

By whom the skies were made formidable and the earth firm, by whom the sky and heaven were fixed, who measured the space in the sky, That someone who is God, let us worship with oblation.

Those vast waters which engulfed the universe, bearing the germ of the world and producing the fire, there He as the breath of the gods appeared. That someone who is God, let us worship with oblation.

He who brooded over with His might those waters which produced the Creative potency and the sacrifice, He who is the One Sovereign God of gods, That someone who is Supreme, let us worship with oblation.

May he not afflict us, He who is the father of the earth, He the promulgator of true sustaining laws, He who created the heaven, He who created the cool and vast waters, That Someone who is God, let us worship with oblation.

'Gods Came After Creation'

The most fascinating expression of free thought is in hymn 129 of Book X. The poem declares that 'the gods came later, after the creation'. It says in conclusion that even he in the highest heaven does not perhaps know how creation has come to be. The translation that follows is reproduced from the Sahitya Akademi's *Ancient Indian Literature*, Vol. I (p. 113):

'The gods came later'

Then there was neither 'what is not'
nor 'what is' : there was
neither space, nor the sky beyond it.
Who moved here, there, where ?
Under whose protection ? What was water,
deep and fathomless ?

Then there was neither death,
nor immortality; there was no sign
to tell night from day ;
that one breathed,
without wind, by its own power,
nothing else was there, beyond it.

In the beginning
darkness was swathed in darkness,
all this was water all around
without any distinction :
the life-principle to be born,
hithérto concealed in the void,
arose as One through the power of heat.

In the beginning,
there was desire, which arose
above all, which was the first
seed of mind; wise men, searching
by the force of mind, found
the bond of being in non-being.

Right across
extended their dividing line.
Was there a below, was there an above ?
There were the planters of seed,
there were powers,
there was self-will, below;
active force, above.

Who indeed knows it,
who will proclaim it ?
Whence has this world come,
whence is this creation ?
The gods came later, after the creation,
who knows then,
from where it has arisen ?

This creation,
from where it came,
whether it was made,
whether it was not made,
the one who oversees this
in the highest heaven,
perhaps he knows,
or he too does not.

How astonishingly open-minded and sceptical this attitude, expressed in lines written more than 3000 years ago. The Rigvedic rishi who composed this poem was content to regard the origin of the universe an unsolved mystery, perhaps unsolvable. Raimundo Panikkar describes the conclusion of the poem as "the light step and the ultimate unconcern of the truly liberated man." Bertrand Russell might have found the Rigvedic ethos worthy of what he called "a free man's worship".

The poem is in striking contrast to the story of creation with which the Bible begins: that God created the world in six days flat, and rested on the seventh day. One is reminded of the remark by Voltaire: "Doubt is not a very agreeable state, but certainty is a ridiculous one."

It is a pity that the bold flights of speculative thought in the Rigveda have not been noticed, let alone acclaimed, by foreign scholars of the Vedas. The pioneer among them, Max Muller (1823-1900), was a Victorian, who lived and accomplished his work during the long reign of Queen Victoria from 1837 to 1901. Besides prudery for which 'Victorian' has become a standard prefix, the times also required religious correctness. Max Muller had earned the wrath of the Bishop of Glasgow for his lectures at Glasgow University appreciative of natural religion, and he might not have wished to risk expressing approval of scepticism regarding a Creator God.

The other two foreign Vedic scholars with whose work I am somewhat acquainted are also cold to the non-theist philosophical temper of the Rigvedic thinkers. T.H. Griffith found the great interest of the Rigveda "historical rather than poetical". He does not even mention the philosophical dimension in the Preface to his translation of The Hymns of the Rigveda. Arthur Anthony Macdonell notes that the numerous deities in the Rigveda share many qualities like power and brilliance, and are often addressed in pairs. Though the idea of One being behind the forms of the different gods was expressed in some late passages, the idea "never developed into monotheism; none of the regular sacrifices in the Vedic period were offered to a single God."

Over the centuries Indian scholars never discussed the Vedic Samhitas critically. Their contents were in fact little known, after Vedic Sanskrit became obsolete by the eighth century BCE. Thereafter only the sound of the mantras was learnt; the verses were (as they still are, to this day) recited without attention to their meaning. Even after Sayanacharya of the 14th century CE restored the Samhitas to life by writing his monumental commentaries explaining each line and word in classical Sanskrit, there was no effort at critical study. The Brahmin custodians of learning were content to accept Sayana's Mimamsa doctrine that the meticulous performance of rituals as prescribed in the Brahmanas is the sure way to reach heaven. The Brahmana texts (written, according to A.L. Basham, between 800 and 500 BCE) were detailed guides to the performance of sacrificial rites, and the Aranyakas which followed tried to explain their significance. Though written many centuries after the Vedic Samhitas they were sanctified as part of the Veda (collective singular) and were passed off as 'belonging to' or 'attached to' this or the other of the four Vedas.

In the modern period, after Max Muller through his translation of the Rigveda in English revealed its light – hidden for millennia – to the world, some Indian scholars have tried to make out that the Rigvedic religion is monotheist. Among them is Sarvepalli Radhakrishnan. Perhaps overawed by the subjection of India for a thousand years by those who professed monotheism, he introduced 'God' into stanza 46 of hymn 164, Book I. In the translation by Griffith, it reads :

They call him Indra, Mitra, Varuna, Agni,
and he is heavenly nobly-winged Garutman.
To what is One, the sages give many a title;
they call it Agni, Yama, Matarisvan.

In the translation by V. Raghavan, the passage reads:

They call him Indra, Mitra, Varuna, Agni, and even the fleet-winged celestial bird Garutman; the One Reality, the learned speak of in many ways.

Radhakrishnan rendered this as 'God is one but men call him by different names'. What is more, he went on to claim: "The Rigvedic seers realised that true religion comprehends all religions." (General Introduction to *A Source Book in Indian Phillsophy*, Princeton, 1957). Can commonality between the divinities worshipped by a people like the Rigvedic community, or between the numerous gods worshiped by Hindus to this day, be stretched to assert commonality between all religions — Hinduism, Judaism, Christianity and Islam?

Looking Deep into the Human Heart

The bold and open-minded approach of the Rigvedic sages to the macrocosm had its counterpart in their study of man, the microcosm. To understand oneself is to understand man; but self-knowledge is not easy. A poet confesses with charming frankness: "What thing I am I know not clearly: mysterious, fettered in my mind I wander." (poem 164, Book I). The rishis were aware of the impulses, some of them not socially approved at a given time, that move human behaviour. One of them boldly confronts the subject of incest. The longing of

Yami for her twin brother Yama, which he does not reciprocate, is depicted in poem 10 of Book X with rare candour and compassion. Given below are extracts from the translation in the Sahitya Akademi's *Anthology* (Vol. I, p. 93),

Yami–Yama Dialogue

Yami: Having come to this lonely island
which spreads far and wide
in the mid-ocean,
I will make this peerless friend
turn to me for a friendly act.
May the Great Creator
after due reflection
place in my womb
the finest offspring
of you, the father.

Yama: Your friend desires not
this friendly act; though we are
of one origin (born as twins).
you are different in build.
The heroic sons of the creator,
the upholders of heaven,
do not approve of this act.

Yami: The Creator himself,
divine and omniform,
made us man and wife
even in the womb.
None can frustrate his undertaking;
Heaven and Earth are conscious
of this, our union.
O Yama, may you desire
to lie with me in the same bed.

I will surrender my body
to you as wife to her man.
Let us exert together
like the two wheels of a chariot.

Yama: The spies of the gods
move around here;
they never stop,
never close their eyes.
O bold one, go quickly
to someone other than me,
and exert in union, like
the two wheels of the chariot.
O Yami, may you take someone
in your arms, and someone you,
as a creeper to a tree.
Seek to win his mind,
let him seek yours, and
make an auspicious union.

Deep psychological perception marks the poem on the Gambler (34 in Book X). A loser who is compulsively drawn to the game, he anticipates Yudhishtira of the Mahabharata who, one moment, rationalises his weakness by invoking the code of chivalry which requires that a challenge should not be declined, and, the next moment, blames 'fate' for drawing him to the dice.

In the poem, which is in the form of a monologue, the gambler bemoans his lot:

When I resolve: 'I shall not play dice
with them (gamblers)', I am
left behind by friends who desert me.

The brown dice, as they are thrown,
raise their voices;
hearing them, I go at once,
like a woman of easy virtue,
to the appointed place.

The wife of the gambler is, like Draupadi, humiliated for no fault of hers :

Others touch the wife of him
whose wealth the winning dice covets.
Father, mother, brothers say of him:
'We know him not, take him away bound'.

In suffering degradation but being undeterred by it, the luckless character in the Rigveda bears a striking resemblance also to Dostoevsky's *Gambler*. a short story believed to be autobiographical. A perceptive critic writes: "The author of The *Gambler* must have understood that it was not hope of gain alone that was sending him to the tables. He may well have been driven by the desire to challenge fate, by the craving for risk, and for the anguish, humiliation that such an experience held for him."

Gandhi was a self-confessed gambler. He wrote in *Young India* of 20th February 1930: "I have been a `gambler' all my life. In my passion for finding truth and in relentlessly following out my faith in non-violence, I have counted no stake too great." Gandhi insisted on launching the Quit India movement in August 1942, when Britain was battling for survival, disregarding the advice of many colleagues including Jawaharlal Nehru. In the prison diary that Asaf Ali maintained at Ahmadnagar Fort where Congress leaders were detained during the final years of World War II, he described Gandhi's August 1942 decision as a gambler's last desperate throw. (*M. Asaf Ali: Memoirs*, Ajanta Books, p. 260). The throw having failed, Gandhi who had conducted anti-war Satyagraha in the early years of the war, wrote to the Viceroy on 27th July 1944 that if a national government was formed he would advise the Congress to assist the war effort – though he himself, as an all-war resister, would stand aside. His offer was spurned by the British, in whose favour the fortunes of the war had turned. The humiliation suffered by Gandhi can be imagined, particularly by his disregard of the Jain doctrine that acquiescence in slaughter is as bad as committing slaughter.

In Lighter Vein

It is not all religious adoration, philosophy and psychology in the Vedas. Poem 103 in Book VII (one of the 'family books' which form the core of the Rigveda), is a panegyric of frogs who break into loud croaking at the onset of rains. There is a good-humoured dig at the Brahmin priests who make a similar noise with their chanting of mantras. Here are extracts:

The Frog Hymn

The frogs having lain
low for a year, like Brahmins
practising a vow (of silence)
have uttered loudly,
their voice roused by rain.

When two frogs are delighted
at the fall of waters, one of them
greets the other; the speckled frog
at the touch of rain, jumps

and joins his speech
with that of the green one.

When one of them
repeats the sound of the other,
as the one who learns
does that of the teacher,
all of them sound
like a lesson that is concluded.

For some of us, shopping is not complete without a bout of bargaining between buyer and seller. It is a duel in which each side feels like the winner when a bargain is finally struck. Here is a battle of wits between an Adhvaryu priest and a Soma seller, from the Satapatha Brahmana :

How much is Soma worth?

Soma-seller, is thy king Soma for sale?
He is for sale.
I will buy him of thee.
Buy him!
I will buy him of thee for one-sixteenth of the cow.
King Soma, surely, is worth more than that!
Yea, but great surely is the greatness of the cow.

From the cow comes fresh milk, from her boiled milk, from her cream, from her sour curds, from her butter, from her ghee, from her whey. I will buy him of thee for one hoof.

King Soma is surely worth more than that, says the Soma seller.

Yes, King Soma is worth more than that, but great surely is the greatness of the cow, replies the Adhvaryu.

And having each time enumerated the cow's virtues, he says, 'I will buy him of thee for one foot' – 'for half the cow' – 'for the cow!'

'King Soma has been bought!', says the Soma seller.

Social Ethics and Transcendence

We have seen that the Rigvedic rishis concerned themselves earnestly with ethics, which belongs to the social sphere of how a person should treat his fellows. A caring and generously sharing attitude was commended, along with the values of truthfulness, keeping one's word, and living in harmony. This was seen as necessary for social health as well as the strength to offer united resistance to an external threat.

In addition to the social, there is another sphere in which the individual, in the privacy of his being, relates and responds to God or the Cosmos or Brahman (the All). This distinction is important. "There are", says Reinhold Niebuhr in *The self and the dramas of history*, "two dimensions of self-hood: the social and the transcendent. The self must both be related to a community and an inclusive historical process, and have the freedom to transcend every social process to seek after unique fulfilments of its own."

Post-Rigvedic thinkers, of the period of Brahminism, employed the concepts of Dharma, Artha and Kama while discussing social ethics. Dharma initially meant caste duty. Over time it acquired the meaning of righteousness. The word is used, confusingly, in both senses in the Mahabharata. Krishna, in the Bhagavad Gita, tells Arjuna not to run away from his caste duty, as a Kshatriya, of fighting the Kauravas.

Bhishma in his dying discourse employs the term in the higher sense. He says that he has been asking people, with uplifted hands, to follow Dharma but few paid heed. In the scheme of Dharma-Artha-Kama as the Three Ends of Man, Dharma or righteousness was expected to regulate the pursuit of profit and pleasure.

Moksha was a later addition, as the Fourth End of Man. The word has carried various meanings: death, as release from the pain and fret of life (the sense in which the word continues to be used widely to this day); as release from the Karma-driven cycle of rebirth after every death; and as attainment of supreme bliss, or transcendence, even while living.

These four words – Dharma, Artha, Kama and Moksha – are not found in the Rigveda. But the poet-thinkers knew what these words referred to. Dharma in the sense of righteousness was known to the Rigvedic thinkers as *rta* (order, both cosmic and moral). Artha and Kama are celebrated in the prayers for wealth and progeny. Moksha can be sensed in the inspired utterance of Vak.

Moksha as supreme bliss may be experienced, as I see it, during: (i) communion with nature; (ii) in inter-personal communion; (iii) during intense enjoyment of music or other art; or (iv) communion with the mind of another, as during conversation with a friend or while reading a book, when we feel the joy of enlarged, enhanced perception. The Rigvedic thinkers celebrated each of these experiences in their poems.

(i) Communing with cosmos : It is not necessary to look high up at a mountain or the stars, to commune

with the cosmos. A flower will do, or a bird, or a tree. To the examples of rapture at nature cited already, let me add a paean to Brahman from the Atharvaveda. The lines are selected from the Sahitya Akademi's *Anthology* (Vol. I, p. 131).

Brahman, the All

Worship to loftiest Brahman, lord of what hath been and what shall be.

All men behold him with the eyes, but with the mind they know him not....

You are a woman, and a man; you are a damsel and a boy.

Grown old you totter with a staff, new-born you look every way.

Either the sire or son of these, the eldest or the youngest child.

As sole God, dwelling in the mind, first born, he still is in the womb.

Forth from the full he lifts the full, the full he sprinkles with the full.

He who knows the drawn-out string on which these creatures all are strung,

The man who knows the thread's thread, he may know the mighty Brahman.

I know the drawn-out string. The thread whereon these creatures all are strung.

I know the thread's thread also, thus I know the mighty Brahman.

This confident affirmation of oneness with the All was made more than 3000 years ago. It finds an echo closer to our time in the words of Dostoevsky, speaking through Kirilov, a character in The Possessed : "There are seconds, four to five, when you suddenly feel the presence of the eternal harmony perfectly attained. It is as though you apprehend all nature."

(ii) Inter-personal communion : Even an unsentimental person, averse to howling brats, can be overwhelmed by the smile of an infant. At that moment occurs a profound mutual recognition. Between two like-minded friends, irrespective of their sex, there can be vibrant silent dialogue in the intervals of conversation. The two almost become one. Transcendence in the man-woman relationship, which comprehends both body and psyche (mind and soul), is thus described in the Brihadaranyaka Upanishad : "In the arms of the beloved, there is nothing inside and nothing outside." The two have become one.

By concentrating exclusively on the body, specially the female form, the modern mass media of films, television and newspapers caricature love, reducing it to lust. Apposite are the remarks of Gerald Heard, an American thinker: "There will probably be no trouble with lust if tenderness is allowed its natural full play. The rule about sex expression must run: always and only with tenderness. In the deepest sense of the word, all sexual expression can be and should be religious. Sex is the possibility of a real communion with life. In that expression, each touches something profounder than his lover. The lover is kissed, but the lover embraces and is embraced by the underlying life of both and all." (The Third Morality, Cassell, 1933).

Significant in the Indian context are the remarks of Kapila Vatsyayan at a seminar on 'Violence and vulgarity in the media' organised by the Centre for

Media Studies in Delhi in 1994. She said that India had through the ages a coherent society which was held together by an application of norms of conduct from within. "The body, mind and soul of a man or woman were seen as one organic whole. But the mass media in our country are now imitating the popular culture of the west which glorifies the body dissociated from the rest of human personality."

She noted that some participants in the seminar had referred to pelvic thrust and gyrations in folk and tribal dances: "These movements of the body are entirely natural in their normal setting and context, not focussed on by the camera long and lasciviously. They coarsen our sensibility only when they are exploited as material to titillate the viewer." Kapila Vatsyayan added that obscene sound in the name of music was not only vulgar; it was polluting, violent and disturbing.

(iii) Communion through art: One does not ordinarily expect philosophy from an artist. But the most eloquent affirmation of the possibility of mukti or moksha (supreme bliss) through art was made by Tyagaraja, foremost music composer of South India whose lyrics in Telugu are on the lips of every singer of South India. Most of Tyagaraja's compositions are in adoration of Rama. He did not seem to tire of singing the praises of Rama's name, form and qualities. But one suspects that this adoration of Rama was an excuse for the composer to explore the contour and shape, feel the texture and enter the mood of raga after raga. The sound of music, *nada*, was Tyagaraja's supreme god.

Is it possible to experience moksha, supreme bliss, even while living in the body? Raising this question in a song *mokshamu galada bhuvilo* (in the raga Saramati), he suggests an affirmative answer in numerous compositions: *swara raga sudha* (in Sankarabharanam), *nada sudha rasa* (in Arabhi) and *nadopasana* (in Begada), to cite a few. Finally, in *nada loludai* (Kalyana-vasantam), Tyagaraja invites us to attain Brahma *ananda* (bliss) through music. There are other entrances to the world of bliss which art opens by resolving the conflict between spirit and matter, and dissolving disharmonies.

The savant Ananda K. Coomaraswami once asserted that religion and art are not allied: they are identical. And the English poet John Keats: beauty is truth, truth beauty. More recently, Arthur Koestler: "When I say the 'I' had ceased to exist, I refer to a concrete experience that is verbally as incommunicable as the feeling aroused by a piano concerto, yet just as real – only much more real. The 'I' ceases to exist because it has, by a kind of mental osmosis, established communication with and been dissolved in the universal pool." In music at its highest the musician, the *rasika* (relisher) and the music seem to fuse into one.

The hymns of the Rigveda, it may be recalled, were meant to be sung during a sacrifice, and the Samaveda was composed to provide guidance for musical recitation. In a popular marriage hymn the bridegroom tells the bride: "I am the Rik (the text), you are the Saman (the tune); I am the Saman, you are the Rik."

(iv) Joy of perception: A poet, a scientist, a composer of music, a thinker, a writer – all these have known, and feel grateful for, the flashes of inspiration which heighten and deepen their perception. The rishis who

composed the Rigvedic poems received such inspiration, says the writer of the eleventh and last of the Valakhilya hymns attached, in T.H. Griffith's translation of the Rigveda, to Book VIII. The hymn praises Indra-Varuna for the gifts which "ye in times of old gave the rishis – revelation, thought and power of song".

After a peak experience there is, in the words of John Keats, 'the journey back to habitual self'. But transcendence is none the less real, and none the less precious, for being transient. K.K. Nair, better known by his pen name of Krishna Chaitanya, has observed: "There is a fallout or sedimentation from the brief moments of illumination and insights. Even when the vision fades away, its gifts can be enduring and can be used to regenerate life."

Jnanam (like *Vak*) is a comprehensive term covering philosophy, poetry, literature and the creative arts. Hymn 71 in Book X of the Rigveda is addressed to *Jnanam* as a deity. Here are the opening verses:

***Jnanam* (Perception)**

When Brihaspati, giving names of objects, sent out
Vak's first and earliest utterances,
All that was excellent and spotless, treasured within
them, was disclosed through their affection.

Where, like men cleansing corn-flour in a cribble,
the wise in spirit have created language,
Friends see and recognise the marks of friendship:
their speech retains the blessed sign imprinted.

With sacrifice the trace of Vak they followed, and
found her harbouring within the rishis.

They brought her, dealt her forth in many places:
seven singers make her tones resound in concert.

The 'seven singers' are the seven metres: Anustubh, Gayatri, Jagati, Tristubh, Dvipada, Brhati, and Irregular. A poem of the Rigveda might be in one of these, or various stanzas might employ different metres.

The poem on Jnanam is best read together with the hymn to Vak, reproduced in Chapter I. It is evident from them that, in the non-theist ethos of the Rigvedic seers, knowledge and perception, creativity in thought and expression, ranked above all else. A sage of our time, George Bernard Shaw, wrote: "A point will be reached in human mental development when the pleasure taken in brain work by St. Thomas Aquinas and the Webbs (and saints and philosophers generally) will intensify to chronic ecstasy surpassing that now induced momentarily by the sexual orgasm."

Rigvedic Values in Tamil Poetry

Echoes of the commendation of altruistic liberality and other social virtues in the Rigveda are found in Tamil ethical poetry of the second century onwards. The best known of these post-Sangam didactic works are the Kural of Tiruvalluvar, and Naladiyar, four hundred quatrains believed to have been written in the 3rd-4th centuries by Jain monks. The terse writing of Valluvar, widely translated, was much admired by Albert Schweitzer for its sensitive reverence for all life and for freedom from a philosophy which thinks that the world is an illusion.

Neither God nor religion is conspicuously present in the Kural, and are absent in the Naladiyar of Jain authorship. The similarity with the non-theist social ethics of the Rigveda will be evident from the extracts that follow. They are taken from Vol. III of the Sahitya Akademi's *Anthology of Ancient Indian Literature*.

Tirukkural

The loveless grasp all, while the loving
With their very bones help others.
He only lives who is kin to all creation:
Deem the rest dead.
The richest of riches is kindliness; mere pelf
even the mean possess.

A sinning ascetic uses his cloak
as a bird-hunter a bush.

Is there a foe more fell than wrath
which kills laughter and love?
Wisdom is a weapon of defence,
an inner fortress no foe can quell.

Let not one spy know another;
And act when three spies agree.
A fool does deeds in a single birth that will
plunge him in hell in the succeeding seven.

(This verse shows that the belief in a Karma-driven succession of deaths and rebirth, central to Brahminism, had taken hold of the south too by the 2nd century CE)

Folly is nothing but the conceit
that one is wise.
Sleepless when he is not here, sleepless when
he is, either way my eyes never rest.
"Bless you," she would say if I sneezed, then
"Which woman?," she would cry, "is it now?"

(There is a popular belief that one sneezes when one is remembered.)

Even close by the briny sea,
sweet water can spring;
And down the distant hills,
might flow brackish water.
Men are not what their race makes them,
men are as their minds.

It's trouble piling it up
It's trouble guarding it.
It's more trouble when the wealth dwindles,
It's trouble if it is lost.
The wealth gathered is always trouble.

At sunset which deludes,
when artisans down their tools,
She gathers flowers
and weaves them into a garland.
She would then let it slip
from her fingers, and wail :
'Of what avail is this garland
to one who is lonely?'

In the 11th century collection of tributes to Valluvar by poets of later times, under the title 'Tiruvalluvamalai' (Valluva garland), there is an interesting contrast drawn between the limited access to the Vedas (which have to be recited aloud with the prescribed pitches) and the free access to the Kural for all who can read Tamil. Gotamanar says:

Brahmins who revere the four Vedas
Recite them but won't write them down

Lest those who merely read them
Fail to achieve the desired end.
But Valluvar's Kural, written down,
Will benefit all who read it,
Demanding no skill in chanting.

Another poet, Vellividiyar, says that the Vedas and the Kural

Both say the same things.
But the Vedas, examined, belong
To the Brahmins who recite them
While the Kural is free for all.

Natural Religion Across Time

Natural religion, which is at the heart of the Rigveda, has moved men in different parts of the world in every age. In England the poet William Wordsworth (1770-1850) found in nature not only beauty and grandeur but the source of moral inspiration. He recognised

in nature and the language of the sense
the anchor of my purest thoughts, the nurse,
the guide, the guardian of my heart, and
of all my moral being.

In the Immortality Ode he affirms:

To me the meanest flower that blows can give
Thoughts that do often lie too deep for tears.

Closer to our time, Joyce Kilmer writes:

I think that I shall never see
A poem lovely as a tree.

A tree whose hungry mouth is prest
Against the earth's sweet-flowing breast;
A tree that looks at God all day,
And lifts her leafy arms to pray.
Poems are made by fools like me,
But only God can make a tree.

In the U.S.A. the poet Walt Whitman (1819–92) exemplified natural religion. "His favourite occupation", a friend wrote, "seemed to be strolling or sauntering about outdoors by himself, looking at the grass, the trees, the flowers, the vistas of light, the varying aspects of the sky, and listening to the birds, the crickets, the tree frogs, and all the hundreds of natural sounds."

In our country Gandhi lived natural religion without knowing it by name or through the Rigveda. Consider his comments in reply to a question on tree worship: "Far from seeing anything inherently evil or harmful in tree worship, I find in it a thing instinct with a deep pathos and poetic beauty. It symbolises true reverence for the entire vegetable kingdom which, with its endless panorama of beautiful shapes and forms, declares to us, as it were with a million tongues, the greatness and glory of god.

"Far different, however, is the case of vows and prayers which votaries offer before trees. The offering of vows and prayers for selfish ends, whether offered in churches, mosques, temples, or before trees and shrines, is a thing not to be encouraged. A personal selfish prayer is bad whether made before an image or an unseen God."

Gandhi said we must so live as to put no partition between ourselves and the sky, "to let the body be in contact with the sky without the intervention of houses, roofs and even clothes" (*Collected Works of Mahatma Gandhi*, Vol 77, p. 35). One should sleep in the open, except in the rainy season, so that one can feast one's eyes on "the different starry constellations" floating in the sky. He who thus establishes contact "with stars as living witnesses to all his thoughts would never allow any evil or impurity to enter his mind." There is an echo here of the belief entertained about the Rigvedic divinity Varuna, upholder of both the cosmic and human *rta* (law, order) that he knows everything we do.

In public life Gandhi the political leader who headed the Congress fight for independence was a self-willed general who committed several blunders: support to the pan-Islamic Khilafat cause; harakiri of the provincial Congress ministries in 1939; and insistence on launching the ill-timed Quit India movement in 1942. Each of these contributed to the growth of the separatist Muslim League and thereby to the partition of India in 1947. The non-political Gandhi, however, was a radical humanist and Deena Bandhu who worked tirelessly for Harijan emancipation and women's empowerment. In drawing moral inspiration from nature, and feeling at one with the cosmos, he was in the line of the Rigvedic rishis.

3

Rigveda Tampered with, Sequestered

Over the period between 1200 and 1000 BCE the caste system appears to have become established. The humane ethos of the group of Aryan tribes constituting the Rigvedic community was supplanted by Brahminism. Based on supremacy of the priestly Brahmin caste, this was a creed which allowed near-equality to the ruling class of Kshatriyas, tolerated the Vaisyas who created wealth through agriculture and trade, and despised the labouring class of Sudras whose lot was to serve the three upper castes (who became 'twice-born' on being admitted to Vedic study). Not only Sudras but all women were barred from learning, or even hearing the recitation of, the Vedas.

Purusha Sukta An Interpolation

In order to confer legitimacy on the caste system with its hereditary and graded inequality, the high priests of Brahminism who acted as thought moulders interpolated hymn no. 90, known as the Purusha Sukta, in the last mandala (Book X) of the Rigveda. This poem proclaims that the scheme of Chatur Varna (Four Orders of Society) originated from the immolation of a primal being in the sacrificial fire. Verses 11 and 12 of the hymn, which has a total of 16 verses, are in the form of question-and-answer. The rest of the poem is narrative. They read as follows:

11. When they divided Purusha how many
portions did they make?
What do they call his mouth,
What do they call his thighs and feet?

12. The Brahmin was his mouth, of both his
arms was the Rajanya made.
His thighs became the Vaisya, from his
feet the Sudra was produced.

If we retain the leading question in verse 11 but omit the Brahminist answer in verse 12, the poem will be like many another Rigvedic hymn expressing wonder at the mystery of the universe and attempting an imaginative, metaphorical explanation of its origin. Verse 13 and 14 read:

13. The moon was born from his mind,
The sun arose from the eye,
Indra and Agni from the mouth,
The wind arose from his vital breath.

14. The mid-region came from his navel,
The sky came from his head,
The earth from his two feet,
The quarters from the ear –

Thus they set the worlds in order.

This is an unexceptionable hazarding of a poetic guess. The mischief is in verse 12. The significance of the anatomical detail is explained in a Brahmana passage of the Yajurveda: "The part of man above the navel is pure; that below is impure" (Sahitya Akademi's *Anthology*, Vol. I, p. 147). It sets out the Chatur Varna scheme which forms the bedrock of the Brahminical social system. The four orders or major castes proliferated over time into hundreds of regional castes and sub-castes in a complex system of graded inequality.

The doctrine that high and low occupations are fixed by the caste of one's birth is wholly alien to the ethos of the Rigveda. It was not to be expected that Indian Vedic scholars would be troubled by this inconsistency, steeped as they have been in the belief that the Veda is of divine origin, the rishis having merely put into verse what was 'revealed' to them.

For anyone who venerated the Veda, it was impossible to question Chatur Varna. Liberal thinkers holding humane values, not knowing that Chatur Varna is a Brahminist interpolation in the Rigveda, have tied themselves into knots trying to defend the indefensible. Even Dayananda Saraswati (1824-83) who has been hailed as India's Martin Luther, and was the first to reject the ritual texts known as the Brahmanas and Aranyakas as wild imaginings and the Puranic tales propagating Brahmin supremacy as trash, tried to rationalise Chatur Varna. He said that the four castes were not intended to be hereditary. They denoted, he held, certain aptitudes and abilities: pursuit of knowledge, and teaching; use of arms for defending society and country; creating material wealth through agriculture and trade; and productive labour and crafts. This is like the claim made by some Muslim divines that Islam being a religion of peace, Jihad does not sanction violence but refers to an inner war by each individual against bad tendencies in himself. These apologetics are unconvincing because the reality of Chatur Varna is hereditary inequality, even as the reality of Jihad is terrorism.

Aurobindo, too, tried to rationalise the four-caste order, arguing in the case of Kshatriyas that it was better to train and use one section of society for armed combat than to involve all in it. Even Gandhi accepted Chatur Varna while rejecting caste inequality and fighting untouchability.

Max Muller in Perspective

It was Max Muller, first and foremost among foreign Vedic scholars, who smelt a rat in the Purusha Sukta almost three millennia after it had been fabricated. Questioning the genuineness of the Purusha Sukta, Max Muller pointed out that this poem, found in the last book, is the only one in the Rigveda to mention four castes, and the Sudras. Some of our cultural nationalists, particularly those who hold to the Brahminism which supplanted the Rigvedic ethos, have questioned Muller's integrity as a scholar. They deride him for having taken payment from the East India Company for his work. They also quote from his letters to show that he wanted to expose the hollowness of the religion of Indians and convert them to Christianity.

The critics do not consider whether Muller could have lived on thin air during the quarter-century it took him (1849–74) to accomplish his six-volume translation of the Rigveda from Vedic Sanskrit along with translation of the commentary thereon in classical Sanskrit written during the fourteenth century CE by Sayanacharya. The commentary was virtually a translation. It explained every word and verse and thus brought back to life India's first literary work which had been all but dead after Vedic Sanskrit became obsolete and largely unintelligible in the 8th century BCE.

The East India Company's interest in financing Max Muller's work was obviously in order to know its Indian subjects better so as to govern them more effectively. It was on this principle of knowing the audience that, subsequently, foreign Christian missionaries and English district collectors compiled the first grammars and dictionaries of Indian regional languages , and devised matrices for printing presses.

As for Christianity, if Max Muller regarded it as superior to Hinduism, he was entitled to his opinion. But as a scholar he must stand or fall by the accuracy of his translation. And no one has accused him of deliberate mistranslation. Max Muller's attachment to scholarship can be gauged from the fact that he did not wait for the completion of his own translation to place before the Sanskrit-knowing public the text of the Rigveda Samhita in Vedic Sanskrit and of Sayana's commentary explaining the meaning of the words. When this project became known, some orthodox Indian scholars were outraged that the text of the Rigveda Samhita was being put into print; some of them in Mahrashtra met to express their collective anguish. In the preface to this work (Oxford University Press, 1890) which was brought out with assistance from the Maharaja of Vijayanagara, Pasupati Ananda Gajapati Raj, it was stated that the publication was intended not for the general reader but "for those European scholars who have taken up Sanskrit for special study, and for those among the natives of India who are still able to read their own sacred books in the language of the original." An Indian reprint of this work, in four volumes, came out in 1966.

Muller is also criticised for his theory of an Aryan invasion of India around 1500 BCE and the commencement of composition of the Rigveda from that time. These critics would have been happy if he had pushed the date of the Rigveda back to 3000 BCE if not much earlier. It is well to remember that though Vivekananda shared this criticism, he was all praise for Muller's great and pioneering work, rating it next only to Sayanacharya's. More recently M.V.R. Sastry, a Telugu writer and cultural nationalist, has acknowledged in an article (Bharatiya Pragna, April 2004) that Muller brought "the Vedas, which were lingering only in the mouths of a few Vedic pundits, within the reach of all, in a world language."

It may also be noted that many Christians did not see Max Muller as an evangelist. In the course of a Gifford lecture at the University of Glasgow in 1888, Muller described 'bookless' natural religion as a religion "which is in the head, and in the heart, and in the sky, the rocks, the rivers and the mountains. It has its roots in the human nature, and in the revelation of the divine." One of its main features, he said, was the sense of the Beyond or the Infinite, without which no religion was possible: "Natural religion may exist and does exist without revealed religion. Revealed religion without natural religion is an utter impossibility."

The Roman Catholic bishop of St. Andrews Cathedral in Glasgow found this shocking: "a crusade against divine revelation, against Jesus Christ and Christianity." Bishop Munro was horrified that a Christian university like St. Andrews could tolerate these blasphemous teachings which "proclaimed atheism under the guise of pantheism and uprooted our idea of God as a personal God."

Max Muller said about Chatur Varna and the Purusha Sukta: "There can be little doubt that the 90th hymn of the tenth book is modern both in its character and in its diction. It is full of allusions to the sacrificial ceremonies and it uses technically philosophical terms. The evidence of language for the modern date of the composition is equally strong. Grishma, for instances, the name for the hot season, does not occur in any other hymn of the Rigveda."

Bhimrao Ramji Ambedkar (1891-1956) was the first Indian thinker to go into the question. In his work Who were the Sudras? (Thacker, 1946), he established that Sudras were originally a Kshatriya clan. A ruler named Sudas and his kin were frequently engaged in conflict with Brahmin rulers, and oppressed each other by turns, the former being finally subdued and reduced to the lowest rank—of a new, fourth caste. This caste is not mentioned anywhere else in the Rigveda. Pointing out the variations in the text of the Purusha Sukta in the different Vedas. Ambedkar asks: "If it had been an old, hoary text sanctified by ancient tradition, could the other Vedas have taken such a liberty with it? Could they have changed it and chopped it as they have done?"

Was it a forgery by the Brahmins to bolster up their claim to superiority? "Priests", Ambedkar writes, "are known to have committed many forgeries. The donations of Constantine and Pseudo-Isidore Decretals are well known forgeries in the history of Papacy. The Brahmins of India were not free from such machinations. How they changed the original word agre into agne to make Rigveda give support to the burning of widows has been pointed out by Prof. Max Muller. There is therefore nothing surprising if the Brahmins did forge the Purusha Sukta: if not the whole, at least the two verses 11 and 12, at some later stage, after the fourth Varna had come into being, to give the system of Chatur Varna the sanction of the Veda."

There is a further point. If the Purusha Sukta was truly part of the Rigveda, how does Stanza 9 refer to the three later Vedas including the 'spells and charms' of the Atharvaveda which came to be recognised only many centuries later?

The Purusha Sukta is by no means the only hymn proclaiming Brahminist attitudes and beliefs. The Rigveda as it has come down to us has about two hundred poems which are attributed to a certain Kanva, of a time later than the rishis of the six Family Books, and his descendants and disciples. Not all of these are stridently Brahminist, many being imitative of the hymns composed by earlier rishis. Book VIII is almost entirely the work of the Kanvas. Other hymns by them are found in the first part of Book 1 and in Book X. The question arises why the Purusha Sukta and other Brahminist hymns, distinctly different in temper from the Rigvedic ethos surveyed in the opening two chapters, were placed where they have been.

As noticed in chapter I, the six 'family books' (II to VII) form the core of the Rigveda. Each a collection of poems composed by a rishi and his sons or pupils, these were preserved through oral instruction from father to son and to pupils. The process of teaching-learning was necessarily mnemonic till the advent of writing around the seventh century BCE. The recitation of the memorised lines had to be with correct rendering of the three swaras (accents) of Vedic Sanskrit. Over the centuries till about 1200 BCE the contents of the six family books become fixed in the memory of Vedic scholars, and these books could not be tampered with. The multi-author books were therefore chosen by Brahminists for interpolation.

Vedic scholars in the west were aware of a certain discrepancy in attitude and beliefs in the Vedas. Thus, A.A. Macdonell in the preface to A Vedic Reader for Students (1917) explains why he restricted the readings to hymns from the Rigveda: "The addition of specimens from the later Vedic literature with their divergences in speech and thought would tend to confuse the learner." While the divergence is plainly discernible in portions of the Yajurveda and Atharvaveda, it is there within the Rigveda itself but Macdonell did not notice it.

For example, the poet-thinkers of the family books were strangers to the notion of an after-life; they did not entertain the fancy that when a person dies, the soul leaves to take rebirth in another body. The individual's consciousness which emerges in infancy, and grows over the years, becomes extinguished with the death of the body. But belief had grown by the time poem 16 of Book X came to be written. V. Raghavan, one-time head of the department of Sanskrit, Madras University, has included a prose summary in his anthology of Sanskrit literature entitled *The Indian Heritage* (1958):

Rebirth

Let your eye go to the Sun; your life to the wind;
by the meritorious acts that you have done, go
to heaven, and then (for rebirth) to the earth
again, or resort to the waters if you feel at home;
remain in the herbs with the bodies you propose
to take.

Surely V. Raghavan knew the difference between the Rigvedic and the Brahminist view of what happens on death. But instead of discussing the difference, he comments that the poem "refers to the beliefs regarding eschatology and rebirth." More pious than critical, he might have thought it improper to see any discrepancy in the Rigveda: is it not the word of God? In the Introduction to his anthology, he writes: "The text of the Veda is absolutely sacrosanct and as the imperishable word breathed out by God, it was the source from which the entire objective world emanated."

Rajesh Kochhar in *The Vedic People: their history and geography* (Orient Longman, 2000) discusses what he calls the 'old matter' and the 'new matter' in the Rigveda. He notes that the first and the last *mandalas* both contain 191 hymns, "suggesting some deliberation". He finds the verses in praise of gifts useful "from a historical point of view," providing "historical data about the families and genealogies of the poets and the princes as well as about the names and homes of the Vedic tribes." He misses the significance of the 'daana stuti' verses that they illustrate the self-serving affirmation by Brahminist high priests about the great religious merit of making gifts to Brahmins. However, I found valuable his location of the new matter as occurring in the multi-author Books I, VIII and X.

My content analysis of these three Books and a comparison with the contents of the six Family Books reveals a clear pattern. The trade marks of Brahminism are found only in the new matter. Thus, animal sacrifice is absent in the untampered Rigveda, it is glorified in Book I, poem 162. Glorification of gifts to Brahmins is a theme that runs through most of the hymns contributed by the Kanvas. Funeral hymns and references to Yama, Lord of the Dead, are found at numerous places only outside of the six Family Books. Separation of Vedic grain from chaff is made easy because the new matter identifies itself through the Brahminist content.

The most unpleasant of the trade marks of Brahminism is animal sacrifice. The report and photograph which newspapers carried on 4th July 2006 of the sacrificial killing of a cock at the Sankara Mutt, Kanchi, was a rude reminder of the almost forgotten advocacy of animal sacrifice by the Brahminism which displaced the Rigvedic way of life. Rationalist thinkers known as the Charvakas, writers of the early Upanishads, Jains and Buddhists condemned the killing of animals in the name of religion. But the high priests of Brahminism defended the practice, claiming that the creatures thus slaughtered went to heaven. If so, the critics countered, why do not the Brahmin priests offer their own parents in sacrifice and thus ensure their passage to heaven? There was no answer.

Poem 162 in Book I, on 'The Horse' is a curious mixture of sympathy for the victim and eulogy of the brutal practice. Here are some verses:

Killing of horse, goat

What time they bear before the Courser, covered with trappings and with wealth, the grasped oblation,

The dappled goat goeth straightforward, bleating to the place dear to Indra and to Pusan.

When thrice the men lead round the Steed, in order, who goeth to the Gods as meet oblation,

The goat precedeth him, the share of Pusan, and to the Gods the sacrifice announceth.

What from thy body which with fire is roasted, when thou art set upon the spit, distilleth,

Let not that lie on earth or grass neglected, but to the longing Gods let all be offered.

They who, observing that the Horse is ready, call out and say, the smell is good, remove it;

The four and thirty ribs of the swift Charger, kin to the Gods, the Slayer's hatchet pierces.

Cut ye with skill, so that the parts be flawless, and piece by piece declaring them dissect them.

Let not thy dear soul burn thee as thou comest, let not the hatchet linger in thy body.

Let not a greedy clumsy immolator, missing the joints, mangle thy limbs unduly.

No, here thou diest not, thou art not injured: by easy paths unto the Gods thou goest.

May this Steed bring us all-sustaining riches, wealth in good kine, good horses, manly offspring.

Freedom from sin may Aditi vouchsafe us, the Steed with our oblations gain us lordship!

The poem that follows, no. 163, is also about horse sacrifice and emphasises the heavenly reward which awaits the victim:

The strong Steed hath come forward to the slaughter,
pondering with a mind directed god-ward.
The goat who is his kin is led before him: the
sages and the singers follow after.
The Steed is come unto the noblest mansion, is
come unto his Father and his Mother.
This day shall be approach the Gods, most welcome;
then he declares good gifts to him who offers.

Cow's sacrifice does not figure in the Rigveda, even in the Brahminist additions. On the contrary, the cow is always referred to with affection and reverence as the provider of oblations like milk, curd, whey, ghee etc. However, cow sacrifice had come into vogue by the time of the post-Rigvedic Brahminist texts. In the Asvalayana Grihyasutra, a rishi says: "To thee, O Agni, by this rik (verse) we offer an oblation prepared by our heart; may these be oxen, bulls and cows.' (Thereby he means: `They are my oxen, bulls and cows which I offer to the gods')."

The Bharadvaja Grihyasutra reports difference of opinion about coronation as an occasion for slaughter of a cow: "The king goes to the assembly. He feeds the Brahmins rice mixed with honey. The priest makes the emperor consume liquor. The king goes to the apartments of the queen. Gargya and Parthasaravasa opined: they should slaughter a cow on this occasion. `No', says Bhagali."

Even after the spread of Buddhism which deplored caste hierarchy, Brahmins and blood sacrifices continued to be glorified, through the medium among others of stone inscriptions. Following is an extract from the inscription in honour of king Kakutsa on a pillar in front of the temple at Talagunda, c. 425 CE. in Sivamogga district of Karnataka. It will be seen that the king is ranked third, after god Siva and after Brahmins:

"Obeisance to Siva. After him (victorious are) the gods on earth (Brahmins), the chief of the twice-born who recite the Sama, Rik and Yajur Vedas. And next victorious is Kakutsavarma, the king who is the moon in the firmament of the great lineage of the Kadamba leaders of armies.

"There was a family of Brahmins, the circle of whose virtues resembling the moon's rays are expanding, which well knew how to dive into the sacred lore, kindled the fire and drank the Soma juice according to precept, which promoted the increase of *Chaturmasya* sacrifices, burnt offerings, oblations, animal sacrifices, new and full moon and *sraaddha* rites...." (Sahitya Akademi's *Anthology*, Vol. I. p. 595)

Another feature that marks the 'new matter' added by Brahminists in the Rigveda is their lavish praise of wealthy patrons who institute sacrifices next only to eulogy of the gods. Numerous poems in Book VIII catalogue the gifts received by the Kanvas; blessings are invoked for generous donors and are interspersed with curses for the ungenerous. Here are some samples:

A hundred necklets from the King, beseeching,

a hundred gift-steeds I at once accepted;

Of the lord's cows a thousand. His deathless glory hath he spread to heaven.

On the high ridge of heaven he stands exalted,

yea, to the Gods he goes, the liberal giver.

The givers of rich meeds are made immortal; the givers of rich fees prolong their lifetime.

Let not the liberal sink to sin and sorrow, never decay the pious chiefs who worship;

Let every man besides be their protection, and let affliction fall upon the niggard.

Dire is his death who pours no gifts; great light hath he who offers them.

The riteless, godless man who sleeps, O Indra, his unbroken sleep

May he by following his own devices die.

There is also, in the additional matter, a preoccupation – not found in the pristine Rigveda – with after-life and with notions connected therewith. Belief in karma-determined rebirth is evident in poem 14 of Book X. This funeral hymn tells the departed soul:

> Go forth, go forth upon the ancient pathways whereon
> our sires of old have gone before us.
> Meet Yama, meet the Fathers, meet the merit of free
> or ordered acts, in highest heaven.
> Leave sin and evil, seek anew thy dwelling, and
> bright with glory wear another body.

Though the word *sraadhha* does not occur, the notion of spirits of the departed receiving food and drink through oblations is evident in the next funeral hymn, no. 15 of Book X:

> Fathers who sit on sacred grass, come, help us; these
> offerings have we made for you; accept them.
> So come to us with most auspicious favour, and give us health and
> strength without a trouble.
> May they the Fathers, worthy of the Soma, invited
> to their favourite oblations
> Laid on the sacred grass, come nigh and listen:
> may they be gracious unto us and bless us.

Given the mixing up, in the Rigveda as it has come down to us, of Brahminist notions of after-life and karma-determined rebirth with natural religion and humane ethics, it is no tribute to Krishna Dwaipayana to credit him with the 'arranging' (vyasa) of the Vedas. The author of the immortal Mahabharata does not need this unfounded claim.

Vedas Reduced To Holy Gibberish

Transmission of the Vedas from generation to generation. by teacher to pupil was in the beginning, before the invention of writing, necessarily through mnemonic devices. To fix the sounds in the memory, the words of each line of a Vedic verse were repeated in up to fifteen modes of chanting. These included: Moolam, Pada, Krama, Jata, Rekha, Mala, Sikha, Dhwaja, Danda, Ratha and Ghana. The student had to reside in the teacher's house and serve him in various ways; it would take some six years each on an average to learn a Veda. Over the centuries, as Vedic Sanskrit became obsolete and incomprehensible by the 8th century BCE, the learning was of the sound only, and not also of the meaning. Even after the advent of writing in the 7th century BCE the writing down of the Vedas was severely discouraged on the ground that recitation with the correct *swaras* (accents), which could only be learnt from a teacher, was all important. Fortunately, some persons did write down the text of the Vedas, despite the prohibition by the high priests. Manuscript copies continued to be made over the centuries. Without this it would not have been possible for Sayanacharya to accomplish his great work in the 14th century.

The existence of manuscript copies is attested by the statement of Panini, grammarian of about the 3rd century BCE, in his *Siksha* that a reciter who consulted a written text was 'a bad reciter'. This warning was because of the belief that only the chanting of Vedic verses with the three *swaras* would be spiritually beneficial. There was supposed to be a mystical or magical potency in the very sound of the Vedas. This might seem to us a superstitious belief. But the belief has been held with conviction by orthodox scholars. So much so that the small number of persons in the country who can recite the Vedas have been rendering the sound without knowing the meaning. To the reciter as well as the listeners it is gibberish, but the sound is considered holy.

In the state of general ignorance about the content of the Vedas, the Brahmin priesthood could attribute to them whatever suited it including the exclusive right of Brahmins to teach the Vedas and to decide whom they would teach. This led a writer in the book-review columns of a leading newspaper to comment: "One must not forget that a `closed-shop' discipline confined Vedic studies to a ludicrously small section of the entire mass of Indian humanity. Nor must one ignore the dire punishment for violation of the rights of the exclusive monopoly of Vedic studies by a very small, though dedicated, group concerned to preserve absolutely and inviolably the almost magical and miraculous potency, both for good and evil, of Vedic mantras." (*The Hindu*, 27 January 1998)

If all manuscripts and printed copies of a Veda were destroyed, observes Prof. Rapson, "its text could now be recovered from the mouths of living men, with absolute fidelity as to the form and accent of every single word. Such a tradition has only been possible through the wonderfully perfect organisation of schools of Vedic study, in which untold generations of students have spent their lives from boyhood to old age in learning the sacred texts and teaching them to their pupils. This is, beyond all question, the most marvellous instance of unbroken continuity to be found in the history of mankind; and the marvel increases when we consider that this extraordinary feat of the human memory has been concerned rather with the minutely accurate preservation of the forms of words than with the transmission of their meaning." One does not know whether to laugh or to cry at this meaningless dedication.

We are now in the 21st century. But such is the continuing hold of Brahminist thought-moulders that Veda *pathasalas* (schools) continue to teach the sound of Vedas without the sense. A report in *Indian Express*, Hyderabad, of 25 July 2006 described the state of affairs in a *pathasala* teaching the Vedas and Agamas (post-Vedic texts dealing with temple architecture and worship procedures) run by the Simhachalam temple administration. There are fifteen students with only one full-time teacher who also acts as principal. Though board and lodging are provided free to the students, the hostel is said to be poorly maintained, and the state of sanitation deplorable. "Synchronised chanting of the Vedic slokas" is taught. What for? So that those who pass out may, in turn, teach sound-without-sense mumbo-jumbo to future students?

Two days earlier the same newspaper reported the inauguration by the State Government at Tirupati of the Veda Viswa Vidyalaya, name of the pathasala there on its upgradation as a deemed university. The Endowments Minister of Andhra Pradesh announced on the occasion that the government contemplated setting up Vedic schools in each district. Should a modern administration do this? If it is intended as a sop to Hindu sentiment, to offset criticism of aid to Islamic madarsas, it betrays ignorance of the content of the Vedas. The primary Veda, Rig, does not teach Hinduism but sets out the ethically oriented non-theistic natural religion of the casteless Rigvedic people, with stress on a caring and sharing attitude in the interest of social health and strength.

It is desirable to propagate the values of the Rigveda, but where are the teaching materials? There is no version of the Rigveda, in verse or prose, in full or condensed, in any Indian language including Sanskrit. The only textbook available is in English-Sanskrit— *A Vedic Reader for Students* by A. A. Macdonell, published in England in 1917. Explained in this work is the meaning of ten poems from the Rig Veda.It is for college-level study, and hardly likely to be useful (except perhaps to teachers) in the proposed Veda pathasalas.

Bible in Konkani, No Veda in Hindi

The way the Vedas have been kept under wraps and hidden from the public gaze for more than three thousand years is in sharp contrast to the success of the struggle in England for the Bible in English, within 800 years of the advent of Christianity.

Christianity was brought to England by invading Germanic tribes during the 7th century. After the new religion replaced local faiths (derisively described by Christian writers as 'pagan') during the 8th century, native poets began to compose songs of Christian devotion. These had some odd features, since Christianity was not native to the soil. Emile Legouis says in A history of English literature that the songs "pictured Judaea washed by the sullen and icy waters of the North Sea".

The songs helped to bring the devout to churches where, however, worship and other services were conducted in a foreign language. Latin had become the language of the church after Emperor Constantine declared Christianity as the state religion in 383 CE and the bishop of Rome became the head of the church as the pope. The clergy of the Roman church did not want the Bible to be translated into the vernaculars of Europe. If distance lends enchantment to the view, so does incomprehension heighten the effect of recitation, specially if the language has the sonority of Latin or Sanskrit.

But those who opposed the papal system and advocated reform of the doctrines and practices of the church wanted the Christian scripture to become available to the people in their own language. Martin Luther (1483-1546) in Germany and William Tindale (1484-1536) in England were reformers and pioneer translators. A humanist who knew the ancient and many modern languages of Europe, Tindale—inspired by Luther's example—began to translate the New Testament into English in 1522. As he was prevented from pursuing this work in England, where king Henry VIII was still a defender of orthodoxy, he took refuge in the European Continent and had his translation printed at Cologne in 1525. Tindale was persecuted and put to death in the Low Countries in 1536. However, after the Reformation was officially established in England following Henry VIII's break with the papacy, Tindale's version of the New Testament became a basis for the 1611 Authorized Version of the Bible.

The intellectual leaders of England and other Christianised countries of Europe did not remain content with bringing the Bible to their people in their own languages. When European nations established colonies in Asia and other continents, Christian missionaries who came in the wake of the traders and invaders learnt the local languages, prepared translations of Christian literature, and established printing presses to disseminate their gospel. The enthusiasm of Christian missionaries has continued unabated in the post-colonial period.

Portuguese Goa, a former colony, is now one of the smaller States of the Indian Union, with a 30 percent Catholic population. Konkani is the local language. The completion of a Rs. 18 million project for translation and publication of the Bible in Konkani was announced in June 2006. Experts drawn from the laity as well as bishops participated in the project.

Contrast this with the fact that standard translations of India's four Vedas are not available to this day in Hindi or in any of the other major spoken languages of the country. Dense obscurity has been the lot of India's earliest literature, about which Max Muller wrote: "Sanskrit literature without the Vedas is like Greek literature without Homer, like Arabic literature without the Koran, like English literature without Shakespeare." By keeping the light of the Rigveda hidden for three millennia, Brahminists frustrated the hopeful prediction in poem 33 of Book III that its verses will echo down time's corridor: "Never forget this word of mine, O singer, which future generations shall re-echo."

Publicity for Chatur Varna

While the high priests of Brahminism kept hidden from public knowledge the Rigveda as a whole, they organised sustained publicity for one hymn from out of the thousand odd poems of the Veda: the Purusha Sukta which proclaims Chatur Varna or the Four Orders of society. For reasons unexplained, this hymn is presented as no. 90 of Book X by R.N. Dandekar in *Sources of Indian Tradition,* V. Raghavan in *The Indian Heritage,* and by T.H. Griffith in his translation of the Rigveda, but 96 by the editors of the Sahitya Akademi's *Anthology.*

V. Raghavan explains how the publicists went about their work: "With a few changes and additions or omissions the hymn occurs in all the Vedas. The version occurring in the Aranyaka of the Krishna Yajurveda is referred to as the hymn of Narayana also." The Purusha of the hymn came to be identified gradually with the more popular of the numerous gods of the Hinduism that was emerging from Brahminism: "The Supreme Being is Brahman. He is Siva. He is Indra ... One of the most popular hymns, it is an essential part of worship whether in a temple or at home, and is recited during bathing (*abhishekha*) of the Image." (pages 10–14, *The Indian Heritage*).

While residing in recent years at Hyderabad I came across a widely used prayer book in Telugu, brought out by the Gita Press, Gorakhpur, title *Panchasuktamulu – Rudram*. The dozen hymns headed by the Purusha Sukta include prayers to Narayana, Sri, Rudra and Ganapati. It is noteworthy that the Purusha Sukta is given in Telugu transliteration, with *swaras* (accents) marked, despite the traditional prohibition of the writing down or printing of any part of the Samhitas.

Indian Sanskrit Scholars To Blame

Responsible for the sequestration of the Rigveda are the fraternity of Indian Sanskrit scholars. A great opportunity for rescuing the Vedas from obscurity arose in the fourteenth century when Sayanacharya (1315–87) prepared a virtual translation of the Vedas, in the form of an exhaustive commentary, in classical Sanskrit. It is so known because it is the language in which the classical writers Bhasa and Kalidasa wrote their plays and poems, and has not changed over the centuries, because it has not been a widely spoken language.

Sayana arrived at the meaning of each word, phrase and sentence in the Rigveda by studying the work on grammar in which Panini discussed the rules of both Vedic and post-Vedic Sanskrit, the Nirukta of Yaska (of about the 6th century BCE) on Vedic etymology, and various Nighantus (dictionaries or books of synonyms). I got an inkling of Sayana's labour while going through T. H. Griffith's translation of the Rigveda. The footnotes abound in references to Sayana's translation of words and phrases as well as to comments of Vedic scholars of the West where, in particular instances, they disagree with Sayana's interpretation; there is no reference to any Indian scholar's opinion. Our Sanskrit scholars have been as indifferent to Sayana's work as to the Rigveda.

'Poorva (early) Mimasa' is the name given to the ritual-oriented interpretation of the Vedas by Sayanacharya. This is to distinguish it from the 'Uttara (later) Mimamsa' as the metaphysical interpretation of the Upanishads by Sankara is known. It is also called Advaita Vedanta though the Upanishads have no real connection with the Vedas. The great majority of Sanskrit scholars and students are from the Brahmin caste. Their 'family Veda' is the Yajur which gives the formulas to be recited during rituals. It is known for this reason as a ceremonial or Hotri Veda, verses from which are recited by the Adhvaryu priests at Brahminical Ceremonies, even as the other Hotri Veda, the Sama, is sung by the Udgatfri priests. Max Muller has observed that Sayanacharya is not an infallible guide since he gives the ritualist interpretation of the Vedas which had become traditional by his time, and not original meaning.

According to a tradition, Sayana along with his brother Madhava Vidyaranya inspired the warriors Harihara and Bukka to fight Muslim rule in the Deccan. This led on to the establishment of the Viyjayanagar empire, with its capital on the bank of the river Tungabhadra, which flourished for nearly three centuries. While this does credit to Sayanacharya, vastly more significant is his bringing the Vedas back to life by making them intelligible. The thought and poetry of the Rigveda could and should have been popularised, through retelling orally as well as in writing, in the people's regional languages, at graded levels ranging from popular narration to scholarly exposition. It is in this way that the central story as well as the subsidiary tales of our two epics, which took their present form in Sanskrit during the centuries immediately preceding and following the Common Era, have come to be known by the people throughout the country. When we think of the Ramayana we recall Kamban (Tamil), Tulasi Das (Hindi), Krittivasa (Bengali) and Eluttachhan (Malayalam). Among notable translators of the Mahabharata have been Pampa in Kannada, Nannaya-Tikkana in Telugu and Sarala Dasa in Oriya. The Puranas have also been translated, notably the Bhagavata Purana – by Pothana in Telugu, Ekanath in

Marathi and Premananda in Gujarati. In contrast, there have been no translations of the Rigveda into Sanskrit or other Indian language after it was made possible by Sayanacharya. Though the script of Vedic Sanskrit was an early form of the Devanagari in which Sanskrit is written, a straightforward and readable translation into classical Sanskrit was (and continues to be) necessary. To say that the Rigvedic Samhita can be understood by consulting Sayana's commentary is like asking someone to read a poem in an unfamiliar language with the help of a dictionary.

Translation of the Rigveda into regional Indian languages from English became possible with Max Muller's historic work during the second half of the 19th century. But this possibility is yet to be actualised. The difficulty is understandable. The six volumes of Max Muller's pioneering translation can be consulted only in the biggest of libraries in the major cities. There was nothing available, in the first place, in any language, to stimulate interest in the Max Muller translation till some 'selections' in English came out in the second half of the twentieth century.

My own first acquaintance with the Vedas was through *Sources of Indian Tradition*, a work of 960 pages covering the period from the Vedas to Partition and after. Originally published by Columbia University Press, New York, in 1958 and re-issued in 1963, it was brought out in India by Motila Banarsidass under the Indo-American standard works programme. Besides American and Pakistani scholars, contributors include R. N. Dandekar and V. Raghavan from India.

The second book I came by is V. Raghavan's *The Indian Heritage: an anthology of Sanskrit Literature*

(Institute of World Culture, Bangalore, 1958) brought out as part of the UNESCO collection of representative works (Indian series). The author, former head of the Sanskrit department of Madras University, presents in English prose the selections made by him of verses from the Vedas.

Then, in the year 2000, I acquired the three volumes of *Ancient Indian Literature: An Anthology* brought out that year by the Sahitya Akademi. The peculiar Urduised spelling is the contribution made to India's three apex institutions devoted to literature, song-and-dance and drama, and the fine arts by Maulana Abul Kalam Azad who knew only Urdu among Indian languages and was chosen by Jawaharlal Nehru as free India's first Minister of Education and Culture. Volume I of this Anthology covers Vedic Sanskrit and Pali. It offers a wider selection from the Vedas than the other two books. This makes it something of a landmark in post-independence publishing in English, though the three volumes have their defects: there is no Index; and the editorial introductions often read as if fellow-specialists are being addressed rather than the general reader.

Selections stimulate curiosity but cannot fully satisfy it. I therefore acquired a complete translation: The hymns of the Rigveda by T. H. Griffith. Without it I could not have identified the Brahminist matter inserted in Books I and X. My content analysis establishes that the Rigveda as it has come down to us has two portions: pristine and untampered, which is luckily much the larger portion and the Brahminist add-ons.

Vedic Cover For Brahmanas, Aranyakas

After inserting the Purusha Sukta and other Brahminist matter in the Rigveda, Brahminists began to write their own texts: the Brahmanas and Aranyakas. The Upanishads, the Dharma texts, the two epics and the Puranas which followed are also largely Brahminist. But in order to make assurance doubly certain, Brahminists did make additions to the Ramayana and insertions in the Mahabharata, as will be seen presently, to drive home Brahminist attitudes.

The Brahmanas and Aranyakas which set out and explain rites and rituals, were written in prose from about 900–800 BCE, centuries after the completion of the Rigvedic verses, upto about 600 BCE. The Brahmanas prescribe the ritual activities in detail, including collection of sacrificial materials and setting up of the fire altar. The Aranyakas purport to explain the symbolic meaning of the rituals, employing myths which are often bizarre. Brahminist thought-moulders claimed that the Brahmanas and Aranyakas are in continuation of, and are indeed part of, the Vedas. The halo of the Vedas was thus sought to be spread over the ritual texts. The poor level of thought and expression in the Brahmanas and Aranyakas will be evident from the samples that follow. The first two are taken from the Sahitya Akademi's *Anthology*. The reader may make whatever sense he can out of the samples.

On the materials to be placed on the sacrificial ground:

He digs the earth to prepare an altar, thereby destroying that which is impure. He sprinkles it with water, with the palm of his hand turned down to pacify the earth. He puts sand over it. This verily is the form of Agni. Only with the form, he takes hold of Agni.

He adds saline soil. It is verily is the form of Agni. Only with the form, he takes hold of Agni.

He adds saline soil. It is verily both nourishment and procreation. He thereby stations fire under nourishment and procreation. Or he indeed positions fire in the consciousness. This, the saline soil, is indeed the sentience of cattle.

Heaven and earth were formerly united. In the process of being separate, they spoke to each other: 'Let whatever is fit for sacrifice be common to us.' Whatever was fit for sacrifice in heaven, was installed on the earth. It became saline earth. Whatever was fit for sacrifice on the earth, was placed in heaven. It became the dark spot on the moon. In placing saline soil on the sacrificial ground one should contemplate the dark spot on the moon. Thereby he positions fire, or whatever is fit for sacrifice, on both heaven and earth. Fire disappeared from the gods. Assuming the form of a mole, it entered into the earth. Burrowing a series of holes, he moved along the earth's interior. That became a molehill. Since the molehill becomes the material for placing on the sacrificial ground, he holds up that, what is soaked of it (i.e. of fire) in the mole-hill.

The white ants indeed heap up the strengthening sap of earth, which becomes an anthill. Since the layer of an anthill becomes the material for placing on the sacrificial ground, he holds up the strengthening sap of earth and also the ear, for indeed it is the ear of earth. which is an ant-hill. One who knows this becomes free from deafness. (Taittiriya Brahmana, 1.1.3)

On how to make a Vedic offering: (read *an offering prescribed in the Brahmanas)*:

One who is going to make the Vedic offering should go out of the village towards the east or north or northeast at a place from which roofs of the village become invisible. After the sun has risen he should sit down with his sacred cord suspended over the left shoulder and under the right arm, cleanse his palms and sip water three times. He should cleanse around twice, touch water once and, touch his head, eyes, nostrils, ears and heart. When he sips water thrice, thereby he gratifies the Riks. When he touches water once, thereby he gratifies the Saman. While he sprinkles water over the left palm and both the feet, when he touches the head, eyes, nostrils, ears and heart, thereby he gratifies the Atharvangiras, Brahmanas, legends, myths, etc. Having strewn around a bunch of darbha grass and having sat down with the right leg over the left thigh and facing towards the east, he should recite the scriptures. The darhhas are indeed the sap of water and plants. Thereby he renders the Vedic recitation full of sap... He commence the recitation with Om. This syllable represents the three Vedas. This is the highest syllable.

Taken from *The Indian Hertiage* by V. Raghavan, the following extract is on the *Five Great Daily Sacrifices*. It is from the Satapatha Brahmana:

Five in number are the Great Sacrifices; they are the great continuous sacrifices; the propitiation of all things created, of human beings, of the manes, of the gods and of the sacred lore. One should make daily offerings to all creatures; thereby one achieves the propitiation of all creatures. Every day one should offer gifts, even if it be only with a cup of water; thus one achieves the propitiation of human beings. Every day one should, even if it be with only a cup of water, make offerings to the manes; thus one achieves the propitiation of the manes. Every day one should make offerings to the gods, even if it be only with sacred twigs (in fire); thus one achieves propitiation of the gods. Then the propitiation of the scared lore; learning one's own Veda is that propitiation. One who understands this and every day does his sacred duty, gains three times the world that is gained by one who fills the whole world with wealth and gives it away.

Finally, an extract from the Aitareya Brahmana which according to V. Raghavan is 'of' the Rigveda. It is a fanciful tale about magical warfare, but has nothing to do with the Rigveda.

The *devas* (gods) and *asuras* (demons) were fighting in these worlds. The asuras made these worlds fortified castles just as the strongest and most powerful do. They made the earth an iron castle, the air as a silver one, and the sky a golden citadel. Thus they made these worlds castles. The *devas* said, the *asuras* have made these worlds castles; let us make other worlds in opposition to these castles. They made out of the earth, in opposition to the iron castle of the *asuras*, a sitting room; out of the air a fireplace; and out of the sky two repositories. The gods said, let us perform the burnt offerings called *upasads* (besieging). When they performed the first *upasad* they drove the *asuras* out from the earth. With the second, they drove them out of the air, and with the third, out of the sky. The *asuras*, thus driven out of these three worlds, repaired to the seasons. The gods said, let us perform the upasads. They performed each twice, thus they became six. There are the six seasons, thus they drove the asuras out of the seasons.

The *asuras* repaired to the months. By performing *upasads* the gods drove the demons successively out of the twelve months and the twenty-four half months. The *asuras* repaired to Day and Night. The gods said, let us perform the *upasads*. This they did. By means of the upasad which they performed for the first part of the day, they turned them out of day, and by means of that which they performed for the second part of the day, they turned them out of night.

Turning to the epics, the whole of the Uttara Kanda of the Ramayana is now acknowledged to be spurious. In it occurs the gruesome episode of Sambuka following the premature death of a Brahmin's son. The death is attributed by counsellors in Rama's court to the practice of *adharma* (violation of caste rules) somewhere in the kingdom. Summoning his aerial chariot, Rama searches far and wide. He eventually finds someone doing severe austerities in a head-down position. Rama enquires about the man's aim, and his caste origin. The man replies, to quote P. Lal: "I was born in a Sudra womb. I am practising *tapasya* to achieve the world of the gods. My name is Sambuka." He had hardly finished speaking when Rama unsheathed his flashing sword and cut off Sambuka's head. The killing of the Sudra made all the gods shout, *Sadhu, Sadhu*! Excellent, Excellent!" (*The Ramayana of Valmiki*, Vikas, 1981.)

The other epic gathered so many interpolations over the centuries that Dayananda Saraswati said we may soon need a camel to carry the Mahabharata. Max Muller explains the vast size of the epic thus: "Every race in the north, the south, the east and the west of India wished to see some account of its own heroes inserted in the national spic. Philosophers claimed some mention of their doctrines. Mere customs, rules about caste, marriage and inheritance had to be placed under the shield of the ancient epic." Even the Bhagavad Gita was not spared. A Brahmin interpolator makes Lord Krishna say to Arjuna that even those "of sinful birth, women, Vaisyas and also Sudras, even they, resorting to me, attain the supreme goal."

As for the Puranas, they indulge in unabashed deification of Brahmins. *Myths and Legends of India* by J. M. Macfie (Rupa, New Delhi) carries the story of Matanga, classed as an outcaste because he was born to a Brahmin woman by a low-caste man.

Matanga resolves to attain Brahminhood by undertaking severe austerities. His penance generated so much heat in heaven that the gods urged Indra to intervene and secure them relief. Indra goes down to the earth and asks Matanga why he was robbing his youth of the pleasures to which it was entitled, and assures him that if he wanted a boon it would be granted. When Matanga asks to be made a Brahmin, Indra is taken aback. The young man would not relent. After several attempts to dissuade Matanga failed, Indra tells him firmly that Brahminhood is a rank that even gods (Indra included) could not aspire for. Matanga had no option but to agree to be made a god. This story was narrated by Bhishma as he lay on his bed of arrows, waiting to give up his life at an auspicious hour.

The entire body of Brahmin-extolling ritualist literature surveyed here has been passed off, by traditional Sanskrit scholars over the centuries, as Vedic and divinely inspired. V. Raghavan has titled the first three chapters of his *Indian Heritage* as follows:

I. VEDAS (SAMHITAS)
II. VEDAS (BRAHMANAS AND ARANYAKAS)
III. VEDAS (UPANISHADS)

The author has chosen as the motto for his work a passage from the Brihadaranyaka Upanishad which spreads the halo of divine inspiration over an even vaster area:

"Behold, it is the breath of the great Being – the Rigveda, Yajurveda, Samaveda, Atharvaveda, Itihasa, Purana, the secret exercises, the verses, the secret doctrines, the aphorisms, the exegetical and recommendatory texts – all these are the breath of this Being only."

It speaks for the credulity of a great many educated Indians that such fanciful claims continue to be made. An edition of V. Raghavan's book was brought out as recently as 1980.

4

Humane Influences on Brahminism

Several major influences served to somewhat soften, somewhat humanise the harsh and caste-ridden creed of Brahminism during its prolonged hegemony since about 1200 BCE when it supplanted the humane Rigvedic ethos oriented to social cohesion and strength.

The reforming agents were: writers of the early (pre-Buddhist) Upanishads between 700 and 600 BCE; rationalist thinkers known as Charvakas about whose beliefs and attitudes we know only from the accounts of their adversaries since their own writings have not come down to us (they were probably destroyed); Jain and Buddhist thinkers who were, to some extent like the Charvakas, rational humanists and who, above all, emphasized compassion which was something new to Brahminism; the Bhakti movement, of devotion to a personal god, which originated in the Tamil land in the south around the 6th century and swept all over the country by the 16th century—a subaltern movement many of whose saints were Sudras; and, finally, self-transcending Desa Bhakti, or devotion to emancipation of society and country, which began with Rammohun Roy, reached efflorescence during the movement against the partition of Bengal, and culminated in Mohandas Karamchand Gandhi.

The influencing was not one-way. In the process of interaction many beliefs and attitudes of Brahminism entered into the body of Upanishadic as well as Buddhist writing. Bhakti as self-centred pursuit of individual well-being, in this world as well as the next, brought together Sudras and the 'twice-born'. But there was little or no lateral interaction between them even though they prayed in the same temples and went on the same pilgrimages.

But all, together, contributed to the transformation of Brahminism into Hinduism, as we know it today, consisting of many strands that are held together by the bonds of geography, history and culture. This ethos has attracted the allegiance of several persons belonging to new religions that came to India with foreign rule. The early Mohammad Iqbal (1873-1938), when he was a nationalist, wrote a poem in praise of Rama as Imam-e-Hind, and another, entitled Naya Shivala (The New Temple) in which he said:

> For me every particle of my country's
> dust is a deity....
> Come, let us build a new temple in our land.

'Hindu Catholic' is how Brahmabandhab Upadhyaya (1861-1907), an Indian Christian patriot, described himself: "By birth we are Hindu and shall remain Hindu till death. But as dvija (twice-born) by virtue of our sacramental rebirth, we are Catholic. We are proud of the stability of the Hindu race. Many a mighty race did rise and fall, but we continue to exist though we had to buffet many a religious deluge and weather many a political storm."

Despite the launching of Muslim 'direct action' in Calcutta by M.A. Jinnah in August 1946, which set off a virtual civil war that raged across the north and made unavoidable the country's partition within a year, India has a very large Muslim population. They live peaceably and are, with some exceptions, loyal to India. What is more, there are Muslim leaders in various political parties including the Bharatiya Janata Party (BJP) which is dubbed by its opponents as 'Hindu-communal'. In view of this, it will be more appropriate to describe the ethos which has evolved from the religious and philosophical interactions over the millennia in India as Bharatiyata or Indianness rather than Hindutva. Though the word Hindu began as a geographical expression, denoting an inhabitant of the land of the river Sindhu (pronounced with an aspirate by the ancient Persians), Hinduism now has the connotation of a religious creed.

Vedanta : Uneven, With No Veda In It

After Brahminism displaced Rigvedism around 1200 BCE, its first interaction was with the metaphysical philosophy of the Upanishads. The writer of one of them, the Chandyogya Upanishad, narrates a story which is a slap in the face of caste-obsessed Brahminism.

Once upon a time Satyakama addressed his mother Jabala: 'Mother, I desire to live the life of a student of sacred knowledge. Of what family am I?' She said to him: 'I do not know, my child, of what family you are. In my youth, when I went about a great deal as a maidservant, I got you. So I do not know of what family you are. However, I am Jabala by name and you are Satyakama. So you may speak of yourself as Satyakama Jabala.'

Then he went to Gautama, son of Haridrumat, and said: 'I wish to become a student of sacred knowledge. May I become your pupil, venerable Sir?'

He said to him: 'Of what family are you, my dear?' The young man replied, "I do not know this, sir, of what family I am. I asked my mother. She answered me, "In my youth, when I went about a great deal as a maidservant, I got you. So I do not know of what family you are. I am Jabala by name and you are Satyakama by name'. So I am Satyakama Jabala, Sir."

He said to him: 'Bring the (sacrificial) fuel, my dear, I will receive you as a pupil. Thou hast not departed from the truth.' Contrary to the Brahminist valuation of a person by the caste of his birth, Gautama ranked truthfulness as the supreme value.

Another Upanishad, the Mundaka, deprecates the rituals of Brahminism: "The sacrificial rites are manifoldly spread forth in the three Vedas. Do you perform them constantly, O lovers of truth. This is your path to the world of good deeds.

"But unsteady, indeed, are these boats in the form of sacrifices, eighteen in number, in which is prescribed only the inferior karma (practice of ritual). The fools who delight in this sacrificial ritual as the highest spiritual good go again and again through the cycle of old age and death.

"Those who practise tapas (penance) in the forest, the tranquil knowers who live the life of a mendicant, depart freed from sin, through the door of the sun, to where dwells the immortal, imperishable Purusha."

The reference in the opening sentence of this quotation from the Mundakopanishad to sacrificial rites having been 'set forth in the three Vedas' is based on Brahminist say-so; it is not based on direct acquaintance with the Vedas. The Vedic Sanskrit in which these were composed had become obsolete by the time of the Upanishads. The Rig, primary among the Vedas, mentions no ritual other than the fire sacrifice. Accretion of rites began with the Yajurveda. They were elaborated in the Brahmanas and Aranyakas, prose texts that were written centuries after the three verse collections (Samhitas) which we know as the Vedas. Yet the propagators of Brahminism have insisted on classifying the ritual prose texts as Vedas, assigning each Brahmana and Aranyaka as 'belonging' to one or other of the three Vedic Samhitas.

Despite the deprecation of rituals by the Upanishads Brahminists have been favourably inclined towards them, even calling them Vedanta (the culmination or end of the Vedas), because they accept the Brahminist doctrine that the happy or unhappy condition of a person in this life is the result of actions in previous existence. This doctrine makes the poor and the oppressed accept their lot as fated, instead of rebelling against it; and it leaves the well-to-do free to enjoy themselves with an untroubled conscience because the condition of the wretched is fated, and cannot be altered.

The test for determining whether a statement or a practice is Vedic is to see if it is found in the Rigveda. The Sama being but a guide to musical rendering of the Rig, the Yajur a collection of formulas for recitation during rituals, and the Atharva not even accorded the status of a Veda till very late, it is the untampered portion of the Rigveda that has to be consulted for authentication.

Applying this test, we find that Swami Vivekananda in his address at the parliament of religions in Chicago on 19th September 1893 attributed the following Upanishadic statement wrongly to the Vedas: "I am a spirit living in a body". No such assertion is to be found in the Rigveda. The mistake arose from the persistent description of the Upanishads by Brahminists as 'Vedanta'.

A second example is the statement attributed in the Kathopanishad to Yama, during his conversation with Nachiketa: "That word which all the Vedas declare, which all the asuterities proclaim, desiring which people live the life of a religious student, that word, to thee. I shall tell. That is AUM. Knowing this syllable, whatever anyone desires will, indeed, be his." The syllable is not to be found anywhere in the Rigveda,

"In hardly any other culture of the world", says Raimundo Panikkar about India's Vedas, "has the fountainhead been paid more lip service but received less real attention. Even the important Upanishads rarely quote the Vedas. Indian philosophical systems, even the orthodox ones, draw very little on the Vedas." (The Vedic Experience, Danton, Longman and Todd, London, 1977.)

Since few knew what is actually stated in the Vedas, anyone could advance his view and assert, 'So it is said in the Veda.' Conflicting teachings have therefore been freely attributed to the Vedas. F.S. Growse, translator of the Ramayana of Tulasi Das (1532-1623), says: "Though Tulasi Das constantly appeals to the authority of the Vedas, it is clear that, like nine hundred and ninety-nine out of a thousand of the most educated of his countrymen at the present day, he had not the faintest idea of their contents."

M. Sundarraj in his Rigvedic Studies (second edition, Madras, 1994) says: "The magic word `Veda' has been the most powerful, if not the only weapon in the armoury of orthodox Hinduism. The Defenders of the Faith treat the Veda as a weapon of warfare in intellectual struggle and also, even more powerfully and successfully, in psychological brainwashing. Hindus realised centuries before any others the superiority of psychological to physical or even intellectual methods in warfare... The ambiguity which cloaks the term `Veda' has considerably helped in these efforts. Far from being a handicap, the obscurity in which the Veda is cloaked has been its most powerful weapon. It has endowed it with an air of great sanctity, and deep and profound mysteries. Not knowing what it really contained, its opponents could only beat in the air, and for its proponents it was magic. Thus it had great psychological value of which Sankara and, after him, all Hindu propagandists took full advantage."

It is, of course, no demerit of Vedanta that there is no Veda in it. The central teaching of the Upanishads has to be considered on its merits: the identity of the Atman (individual self or consciousness) and Brahman (the All). There is a seeming resemblance here to the Rigvedic celebration of communion with the cosmos. But the Rigveda refers to a felt experience, whereas the Upanishads make an intellectual affirmation of the oneness of Atman and Brahman as if they are made of the same substance. If the statement made repeatedly that each Atman is identical with Brahman is taken literally, then every human being should feel towards others 'I am thou' since the same Brahman is in all, and act accordingly. Take the case of a terrorist moved by fanatical monotheistic zeal to kill innocent people. Can a threatened victim be expected to entertain unilateral love towards the terrorist in accordance with the Upanishadic doctrine?

The Upanishads are best known for the four Great Affirmations, one of them occurs in the course of conversation between the sage Uddalaka Aruni and his son Svetaketu. "Bring the fruit of the Nyagrodha tree", the father tells his son. "Here, Sir." "Open it." "It is opened, Sir." "What do you see?" "Sir, I see seeds, as small as atoms." "Split one of these." "One is split, Sir." "What do you see inside?" "Nothing, Sir."

"My dear," the father told Svetaketu, "from that minute source which you cannot see, this huge Nyagrodha springs. That which is the subtle essence, this world has for its self. That is true. That is the self.

That art thou (*tat tvam asi*), Svetaketu." A grand poetic affirmation, even if difficult to comprehend.

Often, a metaphysical statement is couched in language which makes the meaning obscure. Consider, for example, this passage from the Brihadaranyaka Upanishad in which the sage Yajnavalkya tells his wife Maitreyi: "Verily, not for the sake of the husband is the husband dear but for the sake of the Self is the husband dear. Not for the sake of the wife is the wife dear but for the sake of the Self is the wife dear."

It sounds impressive, but is the reference to Yajnavalkya's own individual self, or that of his wife, or to the supreme self (Brahman)? Perhaps it hardly matters, since all three are declared to be identical in Advaita Vedanta, the name given to the interpretation of Upanishadic philosophy by Sankara (788-820 CE).

There is a disconcerting descent from the sublime to the ridiculous in the further statements that follow: "Not for the sake of the sons are the sons dear but for the sake of the Self are the sons dear; not for the sake of wealth is wealth dear....; not for the sake of the cattle.....; not for the sake of the gods are the gods dear.....; not for the sake of the Vedas are the Vedas dear but for the sake of the Self are the Vedas dear." This borders on what has been called metaphysical hallucination.

Equally hard to take for a rational mind is the unqualified non-dualist stand of Advaita Vedanta, according to which the perceived external world is unreal. Just as, says a commentator, dream and magic, or an illusory city in the sky, are seen to be unreal, so also is this whole universe known by the wise to be unreal. Again, a rope that is not well ascertained in its true reality is imagined, in hazy darkness, as a snake, a line of water, or a stick. A comment by Arun Shourie is apposite: "Even the Advaitins never lived up to the pure doctrine they said the Upanishads preached. If the world was indeed unreal, if their bodies were unreal, why were they continuing to eat and drink, to feed what isn't there; if all was indeed an undifferentiated pure consciousness why did they, who were not, continue to teach a doctrine that wasn't either. Where is the scope for ethics, where is the scope for urging us to look at and help alleviate the privations of our fellowmen?" (Hinduism; essence and consequence, pp. 191, 211).

Some of the statements made in the minor Upanishads are amusing. We are told in the Prasna Upanishad that those who indulge in passion during the day waste away prana, while giving play to passion at night is as good as celibacy. The Vishnu Dharma Upapurana says: "Subjugation of the mind is achieved by liberal gifts of gold, bathing in holy waters, hearing holy scriptures, service to one's guru:" A commentator adds, "and ceasing from looking at and touching women." The Upanishads have enjoyed a high standing, because of the ecstatic praise by the German philosopher Arthur Schopenhauer, and the influence they have exerted on modern thinkers like Aldous Huxley (The Perennial Philosophy) and Somerset Maugham whose Razor's Edge echoes the Kathopanishad: `Sharp as the edges of a razor and hard to cross, difficult to tread, is the path declared by the sages'. While the Upanishads have been over-rated, the Rigveda has not even begun to be rated. Its contents have been known to so few.

In contrast to the metaphysical tenor of the early Upanishads, the later Upanishads are theistic. They are a bridge between the naturalistic Vedic divinities and the anthropomorphic gods and goddesses of later Hinduism. Thus the Svetasvatara Upanishad hails Rudra as manifested Brahman or personal Isvara and prays to him for favours, even while speaking of his immanence in the cosmos. Following are some extracts:

> Rudra is one, there is no place for a second, who rules all these worlds with his ruling powers. He, the protector, after creating all world, withdraws them at the end of time.
>
> He who is the source and origin of the gods, the ruler of all, Rudra, the great seer, may he endow us with clear understanding.
>
> Rudra, your body which is auspicious, unterrifying, showing no evil – with that most benign body, O dweller in the mountains, look upon (manifest yourself to) us. You are the dark-blue bird, you are the green parrot with red eyes... You are the cloud with the lightning in its womb. You are the seasons and the seas.
>
> He who is in the faces, heads and necks of all, who dwells in the cave (of the heart) of all beings, he is the Lord and the omnipresent Siva.
>
> Two birds, companions who are always united, cling to the self-same tree. Of the two,

one eats the sweet fruit, and the other looks on without eating.

A person immersed in the sorrows of the world is deluded and grieves on account of his helplessness. When he sees the other, the Lord and his greatness, he becomes freed from the sorrow.

Rudra, hurt us not in my child or grandchild, hurt us not in my life, hurt us not in my cattle. Slay not our heroes in your wrath, for we call on you always with oblations.

Charvaka Materialists

While going through the Upanishads, one sometimes has the curious sensation of being exposed to one side of a debate on the rational or materialist view of the world and of life.

Yama tells Nachiketa in the Kathopanishad: "What lies beyond shines not to the simple-minded, careless person who is deluded by the glamour of wealth. Thinking `this world exists, there is no other' he falls again and again into my power." Closely allied to this is a warning against preferring the pleasant to the good. Yama says, "Different is the good, and different, indeed, is the pleasant. Of these two, it is well for him who takes hold of the good, but he who chooses the pleasant, fails of his aim. Both the good and the pleasant approach a man. The wise man chooses the good in preference to the pleasant. The simple-minded, for the sake of worldly well-being, prefers the pleasant." We do not have in their own words the views of the other unnamed party to the controversy.

Light is shed on the subject by some of the writers in an anthology on Charvaka/Lokayata published by the Indian Council of Philosophical Research in 1990. It was edited by Debiprasad Chattopadhyaya, a Marxist scholar, in collaboration with Mrinal Kanti Gangopadhyaya. We learn from the book that the Upanishad writers were engaged in polemics with the Sharvaka exponents of rationalist and materialist thought.

In the Chandogya Upanishad, regarded as pre-Buddhist and of the 7th century BCE, the view that the body is identical with the self is attributed to Virochana, an asura (demon). Both he and Indra, leader of the gods (let it be remembered that asuras and suras are like cousins) had approached Prajapati for instruction in knowledge. They leave at one point, but whereas Indra came back to Prajapati for further instruction, Virochana did not, and the advantage went to the gods. Maitri, a later Upanishad, refers to a legend that Brhaspati, who like Prajapati was a mentor of both camps, deliberately propagated 'false knowledge' – this worldly, rationalist – among the asuras in order to bring about their downfall. Because of this role of Brhaspati, the Lokayata or this-worldly viewpoint is also known as Brahaspatya.

A Buddhist text, the 'Samana Phala Sutta', surveys the views of the most prominent 'heretics' or non-conformists of Buddha's time. It quotes Ajita Kesakambali (of the garment of hair), who appears to have been close to the rationalist position, as saying: "There is no such thing as alms or sacrifices or offering. There is neither fruit nor result of good or evil deeds.

When a human being dies, the earthy in him returns and relapses to earth, the fluid to the water, the heat to the fire, the wind to the air; and his faculties pass into space. The four bearers, or the bier as a fifth, take his dead body away. Fools and wise alike, on the dissolution of the body, are cut off, annihilated, and after death they are not."

Brahminist texts attribute to Charvakas statements which there is no means of verifying whether they were really made, and caricature them as being reckless in the pursuit of pleasure: "While a man lives, let him live merrily, let him borrow money, and swallow clarified butter." Debiprasad's anthology includes an article by J. Muir, first published in 1861, which surveys the references to the Charvaka view found in: (i) Madhava Acharya's Sarva Darsana Sangraha, a concise account of the different philosophies of India, both orthodox and heretical; (ii) the Ramayana and Mahabharata; and (iii) the Puranas.

Following are extracts relating to Charvaka-Lokayata: from Madhava Acharya's work:

"There is no heaven, no final liberation, no soul which continues to exist in another world; nor any ceremonies of castes or orders which are productive of future reward. The Agnihotra sacrifice, the three Vedas (read Brahmanas and Aranyakas which Brahminists falsely described as Vedas), the mendicant's triple staff, and the practice of smearing oneself with ashes, are only means of livelihood ordained by the Creator for men who have neither understanding nor energy. If it be true that an animal slaughtered at the Jyotistoma sacrifice is in consequence exalted to heaven, why does not the worshipper immolate his own father?

"If a sraadhha (offering of food to the manes) satiates even defunct creatures, it is quite superfluous to furnish people who are setting out upon a journey with any provisions, as their friends who remain behind can offer food to them. Since, as you say, persons in heaven are filled with oblations presented upon earth, why is not food similarly offered by those below to people on the roof of the house?

"While a man lives, let him live merrily, let him borrow money and swallow clarified butter (ghee). How can a body return to earth after it has been reduced to ashes? Ceremonies for the dead are a mere means of livelihood devised by the Brahmins, and nothing else."

In the Ramayana

When Bharata tries to persuade Rama not to proceed further south into the forest, but to return to Ayodhya and rule over Dasaratha's kingdom, a Brahmin named Javali advises Rama not to bother about keeping the word given by his father to Kaikeyi:

"How can any one person be of kin to any other, seeing that every creature is born alone and dies alone? You, most excellent of men, ought not, by abandoning your paternal kingdom, to enter upon a wrong road, painful, uneven and beset with troubles. Permit yourself to be enthroned in opulent Ayodhya.

"A father is nothing more than the seed of a creature, his seminal principle and blood combined with the seminal substance of the mother—such is a man's terrestrial generation. That monarch has gone to the place to which he had to go.... Allow yourself to be persuaded by Bharata, and accept the kingdom."

We are told that when Rama heard this discourse, although slow to become wrathful, he was greatly incensed at being exhorted to atheism.

In the Mahabharata

After Yudhishtira had entered the city of Hastinapura and bestowed largesse on the Brahmins, Charvaka the rakshasa (demon), in the disguise of a Brahmin, addressed the King. This friend of Duryodhana, concealed under the garb of a mendicant with a rosary, a lock of hair on his crown, and a triple staff, impudent and fearless, surrounded by all the Brahmins exceeding a thousand in number who were anxious to utter their benedictions, this wretch, wishing evil to the magnanimous Pandavas, without saluting those Brahmins, thus addressed the King:

"All these Brahmins exclaim, `Woe to you, wicked king, the slayer pf your kindred. What can be the issue of this, son of Kunti? Since you have slaughtered your kinsmen and elders, death is desirable for you, and not life'."

Hearing this speech of the wicked rakshasa the Brahmins were pained and indignant, being maligned by his words. But they, as well as King Yudhistira, all remained silent, being ashamed and cut to the heart. Then Yudhishtira said: "Let all your reverences be reconciled to me, who bows down and supplicates you: you ought not to curse me who has undergone such great misfortunes."

All the Brahmins then exclaimed: "We never uttered the words imputed to us. May your Majesty enjoy prosperity." Then these noble-minded Brahmins recognised the pretended mendicant by the eye of knowledge, and exclaimed: "This is the rakshasa called Charvaka, friend of Duryodhana; in the garb of a vagrant he seeks to accomplish the purpose of your enemy. May prosperity attend you and your brothers."

Then all these pure Brahmins, infuriated with anger, uttering menaces, slew with curses the wicked rakshasa, who fell down, burnt up by the bolt of Indra.

Interaction with Jainism and Buddhism

Jain and Buddhist teachers were, like the Charvakas, rationalists, A. L. Basham says in *Sources of Indian Tradition* (p. 78): "Jainism, though not denying the existence of superhuman beings, is fundamentally atheistic. It never compromised with theism, or devised a pantheon of substitute gods, as did Mahayana Buddhism. From the earliest times to the present day, Jains have strenuously rejected the doctrine that the universe is created or guided by a divine will or a divine mind: for them natural law is a sufficient explanation."

Following are some lines from the *Mahapurana* (Great Legend) composed by Jinasena:

Some foolish men declare that Creator made the world.

If God created the world, where was he before creation?

If he is ever perfect and complete, how could the will to create have arisen in him?

God commits great sin slaying the children whom he himself created.

If you say that he slays only to destroy evil beings, why did he create them in the first place?

Know that the world is uncreated, as time itself is, without beginning and end.

Buddhism too was critical of Brahminist doctrines. A refutation of the claim that Atman and Brahman are one is contained in Sutta-Pitaka (Dialogues of the Buddha) which reports the Master as saying (Sahitya Akademi's *Anthology*, Vol. I, p. 448):

"Just, Vasettha, as if a man should say, `How I long for, how I love, the most beautiful woman in this land!'

And people should ask him, 'Well. good friend, this most beautiful woman in the land, whom you thus love and long for, do you know whether she is a noble lady or a Brahmin woman, or of the trader class, or a Sudra?

But when so asked he should answer: 'No'.

And then people should say to him, 'So then, good friend, whom you know not, neither have seen her, do you love and long for?'

And when so asked, he should answer, 'Yes'. Now what think you, Vasettha ? Would it not turn out that the talk of that man was foolish talk?"

Jain and Buddhist teachers, because they were rationalists like the Charvakas, came under attack by Brahminists, especially in the Puranas.

In the Vishnu Purana, the writer describes how Mayamoha, the great impersonated Delusion, seduced a group of Daityas (standing here for heretical Indians) into embracing Jaina and Buddhist doctrines. "The Great Deceiver", he goes on, "practising illusion, next beguiled other Daityas by means of many other sorts of heresy. In a very short time the Asuras (Daityas), deluded by the Deceiver, abandoned the entire system founded on the ordinances of the triple Veda (read Brahmanas and Aranyakas). Some reviled the Vedas, others the gods, others the ceremonial of sacrifice, and others the Brahmins.

"Thus by numerous methods the Daityas were unsettled by the great Deceiver, so that none of them regarded the triple Vedas with favour any longer. When the Daityas had entered this path of error, the deities mustered all their energies and approached to battle. Then followed a combat between the gods and Asuras, and the latter, who had abandoned the right road, were smitten by the former. In previous times they had been defended by the armour of righteousness which they bore, but when that had been destroyed, they too perished."

Another Puranic story carries a grim warning against 'the sin of speaking to a heretic'. There was a king, the story goes, of genuine piety and devotion. And yet one day as he and his wife came out of the river Ganges, in which they had been bathing, they happened to meet a heretic, who was a friend of the king's instructor in archery. Out of courtesy the monarch engaged shortly in conversation. But the queen was wiser. She turned her eyes away from the heretic and fixed them on the sun.

"Because of the sin he had committed, that is, speaking to an unbeliever, the king was in his next life born as a dog and thereafter, successively, as a jackal, wolf, vulture, crow and peacock. Release came for him only when, as a peacock, he happened to be bathed at a horse sacrifice, after which his next birth was as the son of a king."

The narrator of the tale concludes with this admonition: "From this story you will see how great a sin it is even to speak to a heretic. See to it, then, that you never speak to, never come into contact with, never entertain one of these wicked men. They have abandoned the Vedas (*read* the Brahmanas and Aranyakas). They put their trust in reason. They make no offering of food to gods, rishis, spirits and men. You will go to hell if you have any truck with them." (*Myths and legends of India*, J. M. Macfie, Rupa, p.190).

It is understandable that Brahmin priests, for whom the conducting of rituals was their livelihood, reviled the rationalists. But should we take as truthfully reported the views attributed to Charvakas by their detractors? This is unfortunately what the RSS chief, K. S. Sudarshan did in the course of a recent Vijayadasami address at Nagpur. Deploring the trend towards self-centred rather than communitarian living in the USA, he said: "They have adopted the Charvaka doctrine which says, 'So long as you are alive, enjoy a happy life and take loans and consume ghee'. The only change they have made is that in place of ghee they have substituted wine." (*Organiser*, 23 October 2005).

The reference to wine raises a question. Is the consumption of alcohol sinful? We have it on the authority of Mahamahopadhyaya Pullela

Sriramachandrudu that Rama, Krishna and Arjuna were not teetotallers: "Great personalities like Sri Rama, Krishna and Arjuna were drinking wine. The great addiction to wine of Balarama, who has no control over himself, is well known. In the Sundarakanda, Hanuman tells Sita that Rama was no longer taking meat and wine, with his mind always fixed in her. In the Mahabharata, Sanjaya tells Dhritarashtra how he saw Sri Krishna and Arjuna in the *antahpura* (inner apartment) when they were in an intoxicated condition after consuming wine." (*Kaundinya Smrti*, Sri Gopal Publications, Hyderabad, 2004).

Our ancestors of Rigvedic times relished the Soma drink and invited their divinities to partake of it along with them on the occasion of every sacrifice. Surely it is not necessary that a good person should be long-faced and cheerless.

Ranganathananda, former head of the Ramakrishna Mission, said at Calcutta on Christmas eve in 1954: "The man of joy, which Jesus undoubtedly was in real life, became transformed into a man of sorrow in dogma. We may find a forbidding austerity in John the Baptist; but the Son of Man, as he himself has said, came eating and drinking, trailing clouds of humour and laughter. By transforming him into a man of sorrow, dogma has turned his religion into grim and cheerless aspects. Only a few great saints have been able to penetrate through this spiritual heaviness. `A sad nun is a bad nun'. Wrote St. Theresa; and she exclaimed: `O Lord, save us from sullen saints!" (Quoted in *Organiser* of 15 May 2005).

The Buddhist all-caste order, in which ordination was open to all including women, was a standing reproach to Brahminism. Whereas Kshatriyas and Brahmins had been mutually supportive, Vaisyas were the chief source of support for the new egalitarian creeds promoted by the two maverick Kshatriyas, Mahaveera and Buddha. The emphasis on good conduct rather than ritual, and compassion towards all creatures, was new and attractive.

The results of interaction were two-way. Sprung from the same soil and competing in the same social environment, Brahminism rubbed off on Buddhism and vice versa. The doctrine of rebirth underlies the remarks attributed to Buddha in the *Samyuktha Nikaya* (Book of Kindred Sayings) on an individual's conduct and its bearing on the next life: "Who are they that are joined to light but fare to darkness? This is the case where a man is born into a family of high degree, be it of an eminent noble, or Brahmin, or burgess ... (but) this man is an evil doer, working evil by deed and word and thought; the result whereof is that when he dies he is reborn after death to a woeful doom, to disaster." (Sahitya Akademi's *Anthology*, p. 489).

Brahmin glorification in *Sutta Pitaka* (Dialogues of the Buddha) is as extravagant as in any Brahminist text:

Mother and father are the Eastern view,
And teachers are the quarters of the South.
Wife and children are the Western view,
And friends and kin the quarter in the North.
Servants and working folk the nadir are
And overhead the Brahmin and the recluse.

Religious mendicancy

Entering religious orders as a means of livelihood, and religious mendicancy, are dubious practices which became common to Brahminism and Buddhism. (The first is prevalent in Christianity, too, especially in Kerala.) Liberal donations from agriculturists and traders of Vaisya community appear to have bred indolence and self-indulgence in the monasteries.

A story is told in the *Vinaya Pitaka* (Vinaya Texts) of a Brahmin who is attracted by the way of life certain samanas whom he observed: "The life they live is commodious; they have good meals and lie down on beds protected from the wind. What if I were to embrace the religious life among them?" However, when the period of entertainment with good food at the houses of rich patrons was over, the Bhikkus said to the Brahmin: "Come, friend, let us now go on our rounds for alms." He replied: I have not entered the religious in order to go about for alms. If you give me food I will eat; if you do not, I will return to the world." Buddha is said to have rebuked the man for embracing the religious life for his belly's sake.

But was religious mendicancy itself admirable? It has promoted parasitism. The beggars who gather at temple and ask for alms 'for the sake of dharma' are not a pretty sight.

Gandhi said bluntly: "If I had the good fortune to be face to face with one like him (Buddha), I should not hesitate to ask him why he did not teach the gospel of work, in preference to one of contemplation. I should do the same thing if I were to meet the saints like Tukaram and Jnandev."

The concept of bread labour appealed to Gandhi: "I cannot imagine anything nobler than that for, say, one hour in the day, we should all do the labour that the poor must do, and thus identify ourselves with them and through them with all mankind."

What is 'Sanatana Dharma'?

It was during the struggle of the Brahminists against the new creeds of Jainism and Buddhism that the expression 'Sanatana Dharma' was coined. Brahminists said that their dharma was eternal, or without beginning, in contrast to the recent origin of the rival faiths which rejected caste inequality, blood sacrifice and ritual. The Brahminists invoked the Veda, referring thereby to the ritual texts of the Brahmanas and Aranyakas and not to the much earlier Rigveda which they kept hermetically sealed in Vedic Sanskrit. Since the Rigvedic ideal of a sharing society based on humane ethics remained unknown, the metaphysical Upanishads composed in Sanskrit came to be regarded as the earliest and highest expression of India's religious thought.

Since 'Sanatana Dharma' sounds glorious, many cultural nationalists have felt tempted to apply it to denote Hinduism, not realising that in doing so they are repudiating Rigvedism which is much nobler and much older than Upanishadic metaphysics. When Dayananda Saraswati denounced hereditary inequality based on caste-by-birth, condemned animal sacrifice and idol worship, his followers known as Arya Samajis were opposed by those who called themselves Sanatanis. There even used, on occasion, to be physical clashes between the two. Sanatanis proclaimed the traditional Varna Ashrama dharma as their creed.

Gandhi cheerfully accepted tradition, but went on equally cheerfully to interpret and reform it – often beyond recognition. He accepted the Varna principle of following one's hereditary occupation, but affirmed: "If we must talk in terms of Varna, there is only one Varna today for all, whether men or women: We are all Sudras. In other words, we must all serve." (*Harijan*, 12 October 1934) Gandhi thus stood on its head, through humanist interpretation, the vicious doctrine of Brahmin supremacy in the Chatur Varna scheme proclaimed in the Purusha Sukta which was inserted into the Rigveda by Brahminists.

As for Ashrama dharma, it meant no more than a description of the trajectory of human life: the four stages of childhood; youth and studentship; pursuit of economic gain and pleasure as a householder; and retirement from active life for a contemplative mode of existence. This was what Gandhi's acceptance of Varna Ashrama dharma meant. It was not a defence of Brahminism with its caste gradation, obsession with ritual, male chauvinism and addiction to blood sacrifice. Gandhi said about the last: "Buddha's whole soul rose in mighty indignation against the belief that being called God required for his satisfaction the living blood of animals in order that he might be pleased – animals who were his own creation."

Vyasa on the Human Predicament

Perhaps no two epics of a country are as unlike each other as the Ramayana and the Mahabharata. In the first, the community is too much with the individual; group morality predominates. Thus, Rama has no use for his wife, since she had been under another man's control, after he has vindicated his honour as a husband and a ruler by punishing Ravana who had abducted her.

The institution of marriage on the basis of the mutual fidelity of a man and his wife is a great stabilising institution in human society. The Ramayana celebrates it. Sita symbolises *pativrata* dharma. Every man other than the husband is for her like a father, brother or son – depending upon his age. Similarly, Rama looks upon every woman other than the wife as mother, sister or daughter, depending on her age. It is assumed that there can be no experience or expression of erotic sentiment between two young people unless and until the parents have arranged their marriage. Is this true to life? Reject pre-marital and extra-marital affections and you banish the greater part of mankind's heritage of poetry and literature. This is why the Ramayana has been likened to a moral fable for children. In contrast, the Mahabharata is for adults.

Contrary to general belief, the highest expression of India's religious thought and the deepest insights into the human condition are not to be found in the Upanishads and the Bhagavad Gita. The mixed intellectual fare in the Upanishads has been surveyed already. As for the 'Song Celestial', it begins with Arjuna, dismayed by the thought of killing his own kinsmen in a war likely to destroy a whole race, launching a tirade against caste miscegenation that will result from the destruction of a race; he holds women primarily responsible for the calamity: "A race being destroyed, the eternal customs of that race are lost; and upon those customs being lost, sin overpowers the whole race. From the predominance of sin, O Krishna, the women of that race become corrupt. And the women becoming corrupt, an intermingling of castes happeneth. This intermingling of castes leadeth to hell both the destroyer of the race and the race itself. By these sins of destroyers of races, causing intermixture of castes, the rules of caste and the eternal rites of families become extinct. We have heard, O Janardhana, that men whose family rites become extinct, ever dwell in hell. Alas, we have resolved to perpetrate a great sin" (p. 53 of the definitive, line-by-line translation by Kisari Mohan Ganguli, Munshiram Manoharlal, 4th edition 1981.)

American Whites dreading sexual union with non-Whites could not have spoken with more racist fervour. That words such as these can be attributed to Vyasa is shocking. Much of the Gita is obviously the work of an inferior, caste-mad scribe. Worse follows in the course of Krishna's response.

After a commendably tolerant survey of the various schools of philosophy prevalent at the time, Krishna commends *sranagati* (surrender) as the best form of devotion – a doctrine found useful to this day by godmen and gurus. Then follows a Brahminist slur on women and Sudras which has to be read in the raw full text of the Gita (and not prettified summary versions) to be believed. The Lord says: "Know, O son of Kunti, that none devoted to me is ever lost. For, O son of Pritha, even they who may be of sinful birth, women, Vaisyas, and also Sudras, even they, resorting to me, attain to the supreme goal" (pp. 75–76, Vol. V of Kisari Mohan Ganguli).

This Brahminist balderdash is obviously not Vyasa's work. It is not in the Gita, which is an interpolation, but in the deep understanding and sympathetic depiction of the principal characters of the Mahabharata story that Vyasa's greatness is seen. He does not view life simplistically in terms of good and evil, but sees it whole, as a complicated mix of impulses and motivations, arising from temperament and acted on by circumstance. Vyasa's contribution to the understanding of human nature and the refinement of moral sensibility cannot be exaggerated. There is in the Mahabharata a strong individuation of character: Arjuna seeks his pleasures without inhibition; Karna is reckless in his generosity. Draupadi is more than the world's first great feminist; she is a very great woman, with strong intellect and impassioned feeling. The chracterisation of Bhishma shows how an individual's sense of right and wrong, or dharma, evolves with time and is shaped by circumstance: he is not a 'type', remaining unchanged through adult life till death. Vyasa's characterisation of Draupadi and Bhishma rank him not only with, but above, the Rigvedic poet-thinkers who wrote on the Gambler and on the Yama–Yami relationship and who having pondered the mystery of creation, left it as unsolvable.

Bhishma prevaricated when questioned by Draupadi on Dharma during her humiliation in the Kaurava court. By the time of great war, he has matured and is candidly self-critical. Mentor of both the Pandavas and the Kauravas, Bhishma is approached by Yudhistira for his blessing as well as for permission to fight him in the battle that is about to commence. Bhishma is pleased by this gesture. Making no secret of his sympathy for the Pandavas' cause, he confesses that he had been 'bound by wealth' to the Kauravas. Not only does Bhishma grant permission, but even tells Yudhistira how he, otherwise invincible, can be overcome during the fighting. Another respected elder, Drona, responds similarly. He too regrets that his loyalty had been won by the largesse of the Kauravas.

This confession of Bhishma and Drona has a continuing and profound relevance. The intelligentsia in post-independence India has been suborned through State patronage. In the mid-1950s Prime Minister Jawarharlal Nehru placed journalists under obligation to the establishment by bringing forward legislation to equate them with workmen under labour laws and thereby virtually unsackable, and setting up wage boards to increase their emoluments from time to time. The University Grants Commission has conferred benefits of pay and promotion on college teachers. Academics have been receiving liberal grants for research and for writing, from 'autonomous' bodies funded by the government in various fields of study. This is responsible largely for the superficiality and sameness in the Indian Press, which repeats the clichés and shibboleths of ruling politicians without subjecting them to critical examination. Books and learned journals are not markedly better.

Touch of Humanism in Smritis

The softening effect of the influences surveyed above can be seen in the Smritis, the next phase of Brahminist literature after the Upanishads and composed at about the same time that the epics took their present shape. Comprising texts on dharma, domestic rites (*grihya*) and sacrificial/ritual, they are described as Smriti or remembered teaching handed down by tradition. This is to distinguish them from Sruti (revealed and heard), the term describing the Vedas proper but applied by Brahminists later to the ritual Brahmanas and Aranyakas, and even to the Upanishads which were composed subsequently in Sanskrit.

There is, in the Apastambiya Dharmasutra, a leap for the first time from narrow caste duties to universal human dharma. Desirable qualities for all the four orders – not only for Brahmins or for the twice-born castes – are enumerated as follows: freedom from anger, from exultation, from grumbling, from covetousness, from exultation, from perplexity; subjection of the senses, peace with all created beings, peacefulness and contendedness – these good qualities have been settled by the agreement of the wise for all the four orders." (Sahitya Akademi's *Anthology,* p. 338)

The Manu Smriti says: "Non-violence, truthfulness, non-thieving, purity, self-control – this, in brief, is the Dharma for all the four castes." (*The Indian Heritage*, p. 137)

These flashes of wisdom occur alongside expressions of caste prejudice and arrogance, like: "What Brahmins, riding in the chariot of the law and wielding the sword of the Veda, propound even in jest, that is declared to be the highest law." Or: "They do not put any religious restrictions on the acts of a child before the investiture with the girdle (Upanayana) is performed. For he is on a level with Sudra before the second birth through the Veda."

There is a softening even in respect of rituals. They become less arid and senseless, and gradually acquire poetic symbolism, in the domestic rites that gradually replace sacrificial rituals. The difference can be seen in the two examples that follow. The first is an extract from the Sankayana Sautasutra:

> The *hotra* (reciter of the Veda) should arrange for two holes to be dug for the wooden swing to be fitted. He should measure a foot-step and the breadth of four fingers to the rear of the mound. To the west he should place the plank with its tip facing towards the north. He should measure four fingers breadth on both sides of the plank. He should have lines drawn outside these marks and arrange to have two holes dug for the swing – first the southern one and then the northern one. The forked poles should be fixed in the holes, and the bamboo should be suspended over the forks. The *hotra* measures the height of the suspended bamboo with his head. If he is short, with his raised hands.

Contrast this sacrificial ritual pertaining to open-air *yajna* in the forest with the domestic sacrament *samskara* of Saptapadi on the occasion of marriage, when bridegroom and bride take seven steps round the sacred fire, symbolic of a joint journey through life, to the accompaniment of the following verses recited by the bridegroom:

> Having taken seven steps with me, become my friend; may we two, who have taken together these seven steps, become companions. May I have your friendship; may I not be separated from your friendship nor you from mine; with utmost love to each other, gaining lustre, with mutually amiable minds, and enjoying together our food and invigorating things, may we walk together and take our resolves together. May our minds

be united: I am the Rik (the text), you are the Saman (the tune). I am the Saman, you are the Rik. Act at one with me so that we may be blessed with a son, may attain prosperity. Come with me, O lady of pleasing words!

Saptapadi is a pleasing part of a larger (and, for our times, needlessly complicated) *samskara* of *vivaha* (marriage). However, there are some among the forty domestic sacraments which are dubious. One is *pumsavana*, for the quickening of a male child in a woman who has conceived. The Sanskrit word for son is *put-ra*, one who – by offering oblations at the annual *sraadhha* – saves from *put*, a hell designed specially for the sonless.

In the early stages of civilisation when food needed to be hunted as well as grown, and forests had to be cleared to bring land under cultivation, brawn was more important than brain. Sons were therefore preferred. The New Testament says: "As it is written in the law of the Lord, every male that openeth the womb shall be called holy to the Lord." (Luke, 2.23). But should we, in our age, promote preference for a male child by espousing the *samskara* of *pumsavana*?

The *samskara* of Upanayana had become confined to men of the first three castes by the time that the Grihyasutras (aphorisms dealing with *grihya* or rites) were composed. This is in contrast to the time of composition of the pristine Rigveda when girls, like boys, were initiated into learning at the Upanayana ceremony. It is important that those who, like the RSS chief K.S. Sudarshan, frequently praise the *samskaras* as shaping influences on our culture should make it clear that they want Upanayana, symbolic of education, to be open to young women as well to young men. Otherwise they will create the impression of wanting to hark back to the days of caste-hegemonic and male-chauvinist Brahminism.

But the basic thrust of the Smritis is not humanism; it is caste-crazed Brahminism. Here is a passage, on the caste-wise age for the start of education and the period for learning the Vedas, from the Baudhayana Dharmasutra:

The number of years must be calculated from the conception. Let him initiate a Brahmin in the eighth year after that. A Kshatriya three years later than a Brahmin. A Vaisya one year later than a Kshatriya. Up to the sixteenth, the twenty-second, and the twenty-fourth years respectively the time for the initiation has not passed.

It will be noticed that no starting age or duration of education has been prescribed for Sudras. They were outside the pale of education, which was at that time education in the Vedas exclusively.

Though Sudras are excluded from the learning process, they are not excluded from the duty of giving alms to persons of the three twice-born castes. "A Brahmin student," says the same Dharmasutra, "a Kshatriya and a Vaisya shall ask for alms from men of all castes."

A Re-look At Scriptures

The frequent occurrence of passages derogatory to Sudras in Brahminical texts has led some to suggest that our scriptures should be examined for the pruning of offensive matter. Gandhi once went so far as to suggest the formation of an authoritative body for the purpose. He wrote in *Harijan* of 28 November 1936: "All that is printed in the name of scriptures should not be taken as the word of god. But everybody can decide what is good and authentic and what is bad and interpolated. There should therefore be some authoritative body that would revise all that passes under the name of scriptures, expurgate all the texts that have no moral value and present such an edition fro the guidance of Hindus."

Adherents of other religions too have felt the same need. Thus, Muslim feminists have sought support in the Koran for their affirmation of equality of the sexes, as against those features of the Shariat, as generally understood, that are less than just to women. Similar is the case with Christianity. Feminist theologists point out that the official theology of the Catholic Church cannot be objective because it is dominated by the perspective of male priests required to be celibate.

In the spirit of Gandhiji's plea for a humane interpretation of the scriptures, Rajnath Sonkar Shastri, a member belonging to the Lok Dal, introduced in the Lok Sabha a non-official Bill on 24 February 1984 "to provide for a review of Hindu scriptures and other religious literature and for that purpose establish a Commission ... with a view to identify and omit or amend such words, sentences, paragraphs, stanzas, chapters, etc., from the scriptures and other religious literature which tend to encourage or propagate hatred, discrimination, inequality, or untouchability among citizens on grounds of religion, race, caste, sex, vocation or place of birth ...."

Among the points made during the debate were:

Rajnath Sonkar Shastri: Whatever is happening to the lower castes, despite the Constitution, is because of the derogatory remarks about the Sudras in the Manu Smriti, Gautam Sutra, etc. If such things are present in scriptures of other religion, those also should be removed. The religion of humanity should be established.

Atal Bihari Vjpayee: Our Constitution is the latest Smriti and we abide by it and by no other Smriti.

Harish Kumar Gangwar: If the portions of religious literature that deal with caste are not deleted, then we will not be able to achieve what our Constitution says. As long as such things are there, priests and Brahmins will continue to take advantage.

Harish Rawat: Whatever has been written is according to the conditions in the particular period in which particular scripture was written. We should disregard the bad points.

Abdul Rasheed Kabuli: I respect the spirit of religious books. The House has no right to discuss them. If we try to change or delete what has been written, we will invite more problems. It is also a matter of interpretation. If there is a wrong interpretation, the book should not be condemned. Sometimes, history books and novels and films also encourage communalism.

Ajit Kumar Mehta: The study of religious scriptures should not be allowed in educational institutions.

B.K. Nair: The caste system has not died. A doctor wants his son to be a doctor, a politician wants his son to be a politician. It is part of our culture.

Banarsi Das: We are all with you (mover of the Bill) in your revolution of ideas, but you cannot do it through law.

Ram Dulari Sinha (Minister of State, Home Ministry): Our Constitution ensures justice and equality. It has special provisions for weaker sections. Government takes cognisance of the activities of persons or organisations propagating religion in the form of publications only when these activities threaten public order or otherwise illegal. It is not proper to amend classical literature. Sutras and Smritis are sources of ancient history. Books of historical value cannot be rewritten. I request Shastriji to withdraw the Bill.

The motion for consideration of this non-official Bill was finally withdrawn by the mover on 23 March 1984, after it had served the purpose of provoking debate on a subject of vital importance.

5

Bhakti: A Subaltern Movement

Brahminism survived the moral challenge of Jainism and Buddhism. But, it could not withstand the popular movement of Bhakti, or loving devotion to a personal god, which was at once egalitarian and rationalist. The greater number of leaders of this movement were drawn from the lowest castes of the Sudra order, long held in contempt during Brahminist hegemony.

The poetic justice in this social revolution is brought out in the lines of Ravidas, a cobbler saint:

"O people of the city! Everyone knows I a cobbler by trade and tanner by caste, one of the low caste, yet within my heart I meditate upon God. In Banaras I carried dead cattle to the outskirts. Yet noble Brahmins now bow low before me, since the slave, Ravidas, takes his shelter in Thy Name."

How the significance of the Bhakti movement is viewed depends a good deal on the bias of the observer.

To V. Raghavan, a champion of Brahminism which had by now mellowed into Hinduism, the chief value of Bhakti is that it helped to dislodge Jain and Buddhist influence: "While South India was still under the influence of Jainism and Buddhism (7th-8th centuries), there appeared on the scene Saivite and Vaishnavite saints known as Nayanmars and Alvars, who opposed these two heresies and re-established Hinduism in its devotional form. The Jains and the Buddhists had adopted the popular language as against Sanskrit, and hence the adoption of the local language by these saints."

Communication with Vaisyas and Sudras who form the great majority of the people had necessarily to be in the languages spoken by millions of people—and not in Sanskrit which had been the medium of Brahminist discourse. It was natural for the Vaisya-supported Buddhist movement to adopt Pali as its language, subsequently and for the Bhakti movement which sprang from the low castes to adopt the regional languages spoken by the common people in each region. That these languages are all derived from Sanskrit makes no difference to the fact that Sanskrit itself is incomprehensible to the common Indian. There is reluctance on the part of cultural nationalists to acknowledge this; so strong is the association of Indian *sanskriti* (culture) with Sanskrit. The fact is that a person well versed in the literature of any widely spoken Indian language is as culturally rooted as one who knows Sanskrit.

In contrast to the sectarian partisanship of V. Raghavan, the historian H.C. Raychaudhuri notes that Bhakti promoted a tolerant attitude: "The most noticeable features in the religious life of the people during the Gupta age (which began in 320 CE) were the growing importance of Bhakti (loving faith in God) and the love of fellow-beings which found expression in benevolent activities, and toleration of the opinion of others. "The historian also observes that zeal for social reform, and solicitude for the emancipation of women from rigid custom, were distinguishing features of the Veera Saiva cult in Karnataka, inspired by Bhakti."

Just as belief in God is not essential for affirming human equality or commending the social ethic of mutual aid, the bhakti movement shows that theism is no bar to assertive egalitarianism or rationalist thought. Basava of Karnataka (12th century) said:

When they see a serpent carved in stone, they pour milk on it, if a real serpent comes, they say 'Kill, Kill'.

To the servant of God, who could eat if served, they say, 'Go away', but to the image of God, which cannot eat, they offer dishes of food.

Sweet words are equal to all prayers, equal to all penances. Good behaviour is what pleases God. Kindness is the root of al righteousness.

Annamayya, a devotional poet in Telugu (15th century) questioned the propriety of setting up an opposition between duty and pleasure, between the electable and the delectable. He questions God on the subject in the course of a poem in the raga Kokilavarali. Having given unoffending man the freedom to choose, is it right to blame him if he opts for what gives pleasure? *Doshamu evaridi ayya* (whose fault is it?), Annamayya makes bold to ask.

Kabir, born in a weaver caste in Banaras in 1440, was claimed on this death in 1518 by Hindus and Muslims as one of their own. The devotional verse he composed in Hindi drew freely from both Sanskrit and Persian vocabularies, even as the content reflected Sufi influence on Hindu thought:

Hari is in the East; Allah is in the West; Look within your heart, for there you will find both Karim and Ram.

All the men and women of the world are His living forms; Kabir is the child of Allah and of Ram.

Nanak (1469-1539), on whose teachings the Sikh religion is based, deprecated the distractions of wealth and family ties, rejected idol worship and stressed the importance of good conduct:

The ignorant fools take stones and worship them. O Hindus, how shall the stone, which itself sinks, carry you across?

Vemana, who wrote in Telugu in the late seventeenth century, asks in one of the sayings by which he is remembered:

What animals are ye who worship stones
And care not for the God that dwells within:
How can a stone excel the living thing
That praise intones?
Why should we the *pariah* scorn
When his flesh and blood were born
Like to ours? What caste is He
Who doth dwell in all we see?

There were several women among the Bhakti saints. Well known among whom is Andal of the Tamil country (9th century). Her Tiruppavai verses are widely sung by young women to this day. Andal was, in her adoration of Krishna, the precursor of Rajasthan's Mira. Bridal imagery is freely employed by them, as also by Mahadeviyakka of Karnataka. She describes in one of her poems the release she seeks from Maya (illusion) and from attachment to worldly things:

> I have Maya for mother-in-law,
> The world for father-in-law;
> Three brothers-in-law, like tigers;
> And the husband's thoughts
> Are full of laughing women: no god, this man.
> And I cannot cross the sister-in-law.
> But I will give this wench the slip
> And go cuckold my husband with Hara, my Lord.

Some of the Bhakti saints made light of the difference of sex. Thus, Devara Dasiyamma:

> If they see
> Breasts and long hair coming, they call it woman;
> If beard and whiskers
> They call it man:
> But look, the self that hovers
> In between
> Is neither man
> Nor woman.

ARTS: SUDRAS MASTER 'FIFTH VEDA'

Bharata's *Natya Sastra* (Treatise on Dramaturgy), of about the fourth century CE dealing with all the arts traditionally counted as 64, is described as the Fifth

Veda. It has been open to women and to Sudras, who had been barred from learning the four Veda Samhitas under the caste-crazed and male chauvinist Brahminism which supplanted the humane Rigvedic ethos.

The Visnudharma Sutra, a late Smriti text, enumerates the duties of the four castes:

For a Brahmin, to sacrifice for others and to receive alms;

For a Kshatriya, to protect the world and receive due reward;

For a Vaisya, tillage and keeping cows and other cattle, lending money upon interest;

For a Sudra, all branches of art such as painting and the other fine arts.

Sudra and women have demonstrated that, given the opportunity they can learn as well as any others. Among the Sudra immortals of Karnatak music and Bharata Natya are: Veena Dhanam; the danseuse Balasaraswati, the singers Jayamma, Brinda and Mukta; and the nagaswaram master T.N. Rajaratnam Pillai.

In addition to classical music and the high arts, Sudras along with others have contributed to joy in daily community life through the temple arts: decoration of the deities with silks, jewels and flowers, *kolam* (rangoli), and goup singing of *bhajans* (devotional verses). In the great democracy of Bhakti everyone could participate in the processions o the festival image, pulling of the great car, ringing of the temple bells and the like. In these ways Bhakti overturned and defeated the arid and ritual-ridden Brahminism, turning it into the Hindu way of life as we know it today.

As more and more temples came to be built on hill tops or river banks at various places, the number of pilgrimage centres grew. Time was when Brahminism was contemptuous of borderlands and of people outside Aryavarta; the Baudhayana Dharmasutra prescribed expiation and penance for those who visited the Vangas and Kalingas. In contrast, pilgrimage was at once adventure tourism and a way of getting to know other peoples. In a celebrated passage, Gandhi wrote: "Our leading men travelled through India either on foot or in bullock-carts. They learnt one another's languages and there was no aloofness between them. What do you think could have been the intention of those far-seeing ancestors of ours who established Sethubandha (Rameswar) in the south, Jagannath in the east and Hardwar in the north as places of pilgrimage? You will admit they were no fools. They knew that worship of God could have been performed just as well at home. They taught us that those whose hearts were aglow with righteousness had the Ganga in their own homes. But they saw that India was one undivided land, so made by nature. They, therefore, argued that it must be one nation. Arguing thus they established holy places in various parts of India, and fired the people with an idea of nationality in a manner unknown in other parts of the world."

Selfish and Self-transcending Bhakti

If those who follow the path of Bhakti—and this is the mode of the great majority of Hindus—internalised and acted on the precepts of the Bhakti saints surveyed earlier, ours should have been close to the Rigvedic ideal: a caring and sharing society, mutualism making for unity and strength to resist any attack from outside, military or ideological. The reality has been far different.

The reason is that much of the Bhakti that we see around us is of the self-serving variety, the prayers being for material well-being in this life and a berth in heaven in later. The well wishing is limited to the individual and his or her immediate family, and does not extend to surrounding society or the country.

The phrases most commonly heard in devotional songs are: *pahimam* (save me) in Sanskrit; *nanu brova* (to save me) in Telugu; and *enai kartidu* (save me) in Tamil. Contrast this with the many Rigvedic prayers, cited in Chapter I, which invoke prosperity both for the individual and for the community, for the safety and welfare of the family as well as the larger community. The individual is too much with himself (and his god) in theist Bhakti; the community is never forgotten in the prayers of the pre-theist Rigveda. This makes it a text of lively relevance to our times.

Unlike falling church attendance in the West, our temples continue to be well thronged. But this does not result in social cohesion and strength, the devotees being isolated from each other. In the words of Krishna Chaitanya, "Alike in east and west, unreflecting, pathological devotion has made man forget his fellow beings." And he quotes the philosopher Martin Buber: "A 'life with God' erected on the rejection of the living is no life with God. Real relationship with God cannot be achieved on earth if real relationship to the world and mankind are lacking."

Newspapers have from time to time reported incredible amounts of money or gold being deposited in the hundi (collection box) of Lord Venkateswara at Tirupati. A recent instance is of an unknown devotee from Chennai offering gold ingots worth Rs. Ten million on 8 June 2006. Did the donor come by the wealth through fair means? If not, was it a case of sharing a part of the loot with the Lord as expiation or as conscience money? Worth pondering are the words of T.H. Chowdary, former Information Adviser to the Andhra Pradesh Government: "We may appeal to Hindus visiting temples not to put any money in the *hundies* because that money is taken away by Government or its Endowment Department. The money should be given to some tried and time-trusted organisation of integrity manned by selfless persons. It is estimated that every day not less than fifty million Hindus visit temples in the entire country. If we can persuade them to contribute one rupee every time they visit a temple, we will have sufficient resources but we must have a proper organisation to receive, account and utilise that money for the welfare of the under-privileged."

Piety Without Ethics

What the English poet Shelley wrote nearly two hundred years ago about the lack of connection between piety and ethics in Catholic Italy is largely true of our country too, to this day. In his preface (1819) to *The Cenci*, Shelley said: "Religion in Italy is not, as in Protestant countries, a cloak to be worn on particular days. Religion is interwoven with the whole fabric of the Italian Catholic's life. It is adoration, faith, submission, penitence, blind admiration; not a rule for moral conduct. It has no necessary connection with any virtue".

Even worse than piety without ethics is devotion, genuine or cynically pretended, to mortals in public life who get deified. Examples include J. Jayalalitha of Tamil Nadu many of whose followers literally prostrate before her; the competitive sycophancy of Congress members towards Sonia Gandhi today, Rajiv Gandhi yesterday and Indira Gandhi the day before; and much earlier towards the original Gandhi. M.K. Gandhi was indeed the only genuine Gandhi that the Congress has had, the spelling of the surname having been purloined by Jawaharlal Nehru on the eve of his daughter Indira's wedding in March 1942 and conferred on his Parsi son-in-law, Feroze Gandhi. The reader can look up in Pramila Kalhan's biography of Kamala Nehru the facsimile of a letter to Swami Abhayananda, of Belur Math, in which Feroze signs his name, in Parsi fashion, as Gandhy. The spelling reform effected by Nehru proved of incalculable political benefit to his daughter as well her successors of the Nehru dynasty. (See pages 184–6 of my *New Era in the Indian Polity*, Gyan, 1996 on how the name of Gandhi has proved almost as powerful as the word Veda.) Without presage of these developments, B.R. Ambedkar in 1943 cautioned against Bhakti in politics.

"I am condemned", he said in the preface to a booklet carrying his lecture on 'Ranade, Gandhi and Jinnah' (on the occasion of Mahadeo Govind Ranade's birth centenary on 18th January 1943 in Pune) "because I criticised Mr. Gandhi and Mr. Jinnah for the mess they have made of Indian politics. I tender no apology for my criticism. I have hopes that my countrymen will some day learn that the country is greater than the man." Ambedkar recalled a statement by Pope Pius IX when a controversy was raging on the issue of Papal infallibility; now I *feel* it.' Ambedkar added: "This is exactly the attitude of the two leaders whom providence—may I say in his unguarded moments—has appointed to lead us."

Serving Society and Country

Unlike an individual's prayer, which can be conducted in the privacy of his mind or home, self-transcending devotion finds public expression, in the form of service to society and the country. As Paul Tillich puts it, "There is no dualism between soul and body. Helping a man is helping the whole man, body and spirit together. When there is only a direct line reaching upward from each individual and the kingdom of God has to be reached by only individual souls, the forward-looking fervour of religion is paralysed and the world-transforming aspect of the idea of the kingdom of God disappears...Religion cannot be a diversion from the political struggle."

Self-transcending devotion as public service flowered in the modern period during the struggle for self-government which was at once stimulated by and directed against British rule. But even in the medieval period when sensitive minds expressed themselves in religious and not political terms, there appeared early in the 12th century a religious teacher by name Ramanuja who broke the ban on imparting a certain 'saving' formula to the low-born. Tradition has it that Ramanuja's guru had given him the seven-syllable mantra (*Om Namo Narayana*) with the warning that he would go to hell if he shared it with all and sundry. M. Narasimhachary, an authority on Vaishnavism, writes: "Ramanuja soon assembled all the people of Tirukkottiyur. He himself took up a vantage position on the temple steeple. He explained the meaning of the mantra and made every one chant it." Ramanuja's guru was first horrified, but was soon moved by the large-heartedness of his disciple.

The writer adds: "Ramanuja renamed the hill tribes of Melkote 'Tirukulattar' (of the family of Goddess Lakshmi) and arranged for their entry into the local temple during the Brahmotsava festival. This was at a time when temple entry for the lower sections of society was unheard of. It is this compassion that makes Ramanuja stand head and shoulders above all the Vedantins." For a student of the social effect of religion and philosophy, this is much more significant than Ramanuja's theory of Visista Advaita (qualified monism).

The first great exemplar of self-transcending devotion as Desa Bhakti is Rammohun Roy (1722–1833), initiator of India's renascence in the modern period. Well versed in Sanskrit (as also Persian and Arabic), he translated some of the Upanishads directly into Bengali. But while being rooted in our religious thought and culture, he wanted that India should profit from the modern sciences, knowledge of which had been brought by the British rulers. This may come as a shock to some of our cultural nationalists, but Rammohun opposed the East India Company's decision to open a new Sanskrit college in Calcutta. He wrote to Lord Amherst, the then Governor-General, that it would only "impart such knowledge as is already current in India." He urged instead that the government should "promote a more liberal and enlightened system of instruction embracing mathematics, natural philosophy, chemistry, anatomy, with other useful sciences, which may be accomplished with the sums proposed by employing a few gentlemen of talent and learning educated in Europe, and providing the college with necessary books, instruments and other apparatus."

This was full twelve years before the 1835 Minute on Education of Thomas Macaulay, Power-hungry politicians of post-independence India who abolished English at school level in the name of promoting local languages (while sending their own children to English medium schools) are now realising that English must be taught from the earliest stage if their States are not to lag behind others in the emergence of Indian as a knowledge power.

Joining the East India Company's service, Rammohun assisted British officials in the revenue and judicial administration at district level. Though a rich zamindar himself, he urged that a limit should be fixed on the rent payable by cultivators. Rammohun was the first to advocate many of the reforms which were to be demanded in subsequent decades by leaders of the nationalist movement, such as equality before the law and separation of the judiciary. He did not demand representative government: it was too soon for that, with an entrenched imperial power and a people steeped in illiteracy and ignorance and with little sense of any larger identity beyond caste. But his consciousness of India's unfortunate status as a subject country and his readiness to assert national self-respect are evident from his courageous criticism of the foreign missionaries' tactics.

"It is true", he said, "that the apostles of Jesus Christ used to preach the superiority of the Christian religion to the natives of different countries. But we must recollect that they were not the rulers of those countries where they preached. Were the missionaries likewise to preach the Gospel and distribute books in countries not conquered by the English, such as Turkey, Persia, etc., which are much nearer England, they would be esteemed a body of men truly zealous in propagating religion and in following the example of the founders of Christianity. In Bengal, where the English are the sole rulers, and where the mere name of Englishman is sufficient to frighten people, an encroachment upon the rights of her poor, timid and humble inhabitants and upon their religion cannot be viewed in the eyes of God or the public as a justifiable act."

Rammohun wanted Hindu leaders to be prepared to take back converts to Christianity who wanted to return to their mother religion.

The early missionaries thought nothing of holding out material inducements to secure conversions. He said in a letter to Rev. Henry Ware of the Harvard College, U.S.A.: "Several years ago there was a pretty prevalent report in this part of India that a native embracing Christianity should be remunerated for his loss of caste by the gift of five hundred rupees, with a country-born Christian woman as his wife; and while this report had any pretension to credit, several natives offered from time to time to become Christians. The hope of any such recompense being taken away, the old converts find now very few inclined to follow their example. This disappointment not only discourages further conversion, but has also induced several Moosulman converts to return to their former faith; and had Hindoos with equal facility admitted the return of outcasts to their society, a great number of them also would, I suspect, have imitated the conduct of their brother Moosulman converts."

The first journals in Bengali, Persian and English were brought out by Rammohun Roy, in or around 1821, making him the father of the Indian Press. He utilised these journals (*Sambad Kaumidi* in Bengali, *Mirat ul Akhbar* in Persian, and the *Brahmunical Magaine* in English) to counter the tirades of Christian missionaries against Hinduism and to advocate reforms in Indian society. On the one hand Rammohun appealed to his countrymen to free themselves from the incubus of obscurantist traditions; to discard the rigidities of caste; to equip themselves with modern knowledge; and to cultivate thrift and industry. On the other hand he kept making demands on the authorities such as for the opening of modern schools; improvement of conservancy services in Calcutta; and making the services of European physicians available to Indians.

The first journal to be printed on Indian soil was the *Bengal Gazette* of James Augustsus Hicky. But it was addressed exclusively to Europeans, not to Indians. Those writers of textbooks on journalism who describe Hicky as the father of Indian journalism are therefore off the mark.

Rammohun Roy was principally responsible for securing the legal prohibition of the custom of widow-burning known as sati. This horrific practice—unknown in Rigvedic times—was extreme manifestation of the male chauvinism which characterised the Brahminism that supplanted the Rigvedic way of life. R.C. Majumdar refers to the accounts by Greek writers of a case of Sati that occurred in the 4th century BC, and adds: "But it was not enjoined as a sacred religious duty until centuries later. The practice is not referred to in the earliest law books, and is merely permitted as an option to widows in later books. The last stage in this tragic drama was reached when the scriptures laid down self-immolation on the funeral pyre of her husband as the only meritorious course that a virtuous woman could follow." (*An advanced History of India*, p. 823). When orthodox Hindus agitated against Regulation XVII of Lord Bentinck abolishing Sati, Rammohun Roy organised a counter petition, congratulating the Governor-General, signed by 300 residents of Calcutta.

The work of social reform promoted by Rammohun Roy was carried forward after his death by members of the Brahmo Samaj founded by him in 1828. Funds for the activities of the Samaj were contributed liberally by Dwarkanath Tagore, grandfather of poet Rabindranath.

Dayananda Saraswati

The greatest social and religious reformer after Rammohun Roy and till Gandhi was Dayananda Saraswati (1824–83). Unlike the other two, Dayananda did not master English; he spoke and wrote only in Hindi. This limited the impact he made on the minds of Indians. There is no getting away from the fact that not Sanskrit, not Hindi but English has become the language of pan-Indian intellectual communication (as distinct from information and entertainment). His life-work and thought deserve to be known much more widely than they are.

Aurobindo was among the few who realised that the Upanishads were not the source of Indian philosophy, being very much later than the Vedas. He described Dayananda as "a pine jutting out into the blue among the great company of remarkable figures that will appear to the eye of posterity at the head of the Indian Renascence. Rammohun Roy, that other great soul and puissant worker, who laid his hand on Bengal and shook her, stopped short at the Upanishads. Dayanada looked beyond and perceived that our true original seeds was the Veda. To be national is not to stand still. Rather, to seize on a vital thing out of the past and throw it into the stream of modern life is really the most powerful means of renovation and neo-creation."

Thanks to the rigid ban imposed by Brahminists on writing down or translating the Vedas (even from Vedic into classical Sanskrit), the Vedas have had to be learnt the hard way: mnemonically. That is the way Dayananda learnt them. The editors of *The Sources of Indian tradition* say, in the chapter on 'The Renascence of Hinduism': "Dayananda revolted against idol worship at fourteen, and to avoid being married ran away from home at nineteen to become a sannyasi of the Saraswati order. He spent the next fifteen years as a wandering ascetic, living in jungles, in Himalayan retreats, and at places of pilgrimage throughout northern India. A tough, blind old teacher completed his education by literally beating into him a reverence for the four Vedas and a disdain for all later scriptures."

For the rest of his life Dayananda lectured in all parts of the country. Idol worship is not sanctioned by the Vedas, he pointed out, nor is untouchability, nor child marriage, nor the subjection of women to unequal status with men. The study of the Vedas should be open to all, not just Brahmins, and a man's caste should be in accordance with his merits. Such revolutionary teaching evoked the wrath of the orthodox and numerous attempts were made on Dayananda's life. It should be noted that Dayananda held only the verses of the four Veda Samhitas to be the word of God. He rejected the much later ritual texts (Brahmanas and Aranyakas), and the Upanishads which the Brahminists claimed were all Vedas too.

Monier Williams, a Sanskrit scholar has left the following account: "I made Dayananda's acquaintance in Bombay in 1876, and was much struck by his fine countenance and figure. There I heard him preach an eloquent discourse on the religious development of the Aryan race. He began by repeating a hymn to Varuna, preceded by the syllable Om—prolating the vowel in a deep sonorous tone. In one of my interviews, I asked him for his definition of religion. He replied in Sanskrit: Religion is an impartial inquiry into the truth by means of the senses and two other instruments of knowledge—reason and revelation."

6

Encounter with Other Creeds

Mohandas Karamchand Gandhi (1869–1948) completed India's re-awakening. It is remarkable that during the encounter of Hinduism, two out of the three outstanding leaders of India's renaissance in the modern period—Rammohun Roy and Gandhi—were profoundly attracted by the Gospels with which the New Testament of the Bible begins.

In contrast, few Indians of note were attracted by the Koran. This is perhaps because a country which had produced the Rigveda and the Mahabharata had little to learn from Islam. Its influence was confined to those who were converted by force including the economic pressure exerted on the indigent among non-Muslims by the *jizya* or poll tax on non-Muslims—following the Muslim invasions from the 11th century onwards.

The converts were almost wholly from the lower castes, to whom the equality claimed for Islam had a certain appeal though, as was to be the case with Christianity later, the promise proved illusory. Any change must have appeared worth trying to those oppressed and despised for centuries under the caste hierarchy bequeathed by Brahminism. The social system of caste continued despite the fact that many Sudras led the Bhakti movement which helped to soften and to change Brahminism.

M. Asaf Ali's analysis of the social composition of the converts to Islam, specially in East Bengal (now Bangladesh) is illuminating. It occurs in the course of his comments on the manuscript of *The Discovery of India* which Jawaharlal Nehru gave him to read and comment on when both of them were in detention at Ahmadnagar Fort during World War II. Nehru had said in the draft: "Since British rule came to India, Muslims have produced few outstanding figures of the modern type."

Asaf Ali comments: "But why is it astonishing? The so-called foreign stock is now said to be ten percent or even less. Since a majority of the 90 percent of the Hindu converts are believed to have come from people suppressed for 2,000 to 3,000 years, the paucity you refer to is natural. Conversion became such a wholesale affair in Bengal because the ruling minority was like the South African and East African white settlers in a sense, with the vast majority of the Sudras and the land-labouring Vaisyas remaining depressed and the untouchables being condemned to a life of misery. Moreover, the lag of nearly a century (Bengal) and in some cases of 200 years (Madras) in modern education has to be taken into consideration. I am aware of no Tagores, P.C. Roys and

Ramans repeated by the other Provinces." (*M. Asaf Ali: Memoirs*, Ajanta Publications, 1995, p. 304)

Nehru took Asaf Ali's remarks into account. The passage in *The Discovery* as published reads: "This incapacity to march with the changing times and adapt themselves culturally and otherwise in a new environment was of course not due to any innate failing. In Bengal the backwardness of Muslims was most marked, but this was obviously due to two causes: the destruction of their upper classes during the early days of British rule, and the fact that the vast majority were converts from the lowest class of Hindus, who had long been denied opportunities of growth and progress."

Hindu Blood in Sub-continent's Muslims

In the sixtieth year of the sub-continent's Partition, following the The Peace talks entered into by India and Pakistan at American urging, a leading Pakistani journalist made a surprisingly candid statement: "The vast majority of Muslims in the sub-continent have more Hindu blood in their veins then there is Arab, Afghan, Turkish or Persian blood." S. Gurumurthy, writing in *Indian Express* of 30th January 2007, quotes Irjan Habib as saying further: "A study and understanding of the past will promote better understanding between the two communities." The ethnic identity with Hindu India is even closer in the case of Bangladesh, formerly East Pakistan.

Before and after 1947, till now, the average Muslim has not liked to be reminded of the historical fact of Hindu blood in Muslims of the sub-continent. Gandhi stated the fact bluntly, for the first time, in *Harijan* of 6th April 1940: "The two-nation theory is an untruth. The vast majority of Muslims of India are converts to Islam or descendants of converts. They did not become a separate nation on becoming converts."

This was after the Muslim League's Lahore resolution, of March 1940, which asserted that the Muslims of India had a distinct culture and were entitled to the establishment of sovereign and independent Muslim homelands in the north-east and north-west of India. Prior to this, Gandhi did not speak of Hindus and Muslims as blood brothers with a common ancestry. On the contrary, from 1919 onwards his words and actions had the effect of strengthening the sense of separate Muslim identity. Why did Gandhi follow the policy of appeasing Islamists over the long years from 1919? Here is a rapid survey. India's British rulers were alarmed by the strength and extent of nationalist opposition to Lord Curzon's partition of Bengal in 1905 to create a new Muslim-majority province of Eastern Bengal. This reorganisation was intended to divide Muslims from the Hindus of Bengal. Unnerved by the nationalist reaction, British officials sponsored a Muslim delegation, led by the Aga Khan, to wait on the Viceroy. At their meeting with Minto in 1906 they told him that democratic institutions of the western model did not suit India. They wanted that Muslims should be given special weightage in the Central and provincial legislatures, and that Muslim seats should be filled by Muslims elected by Muslims only as a separate electorate. The Indian Councils Act of 1909 introduced separate electorates for Muslims, spreading over the whole of India the mischief underlying the partition of Bengal. The annulment of Bengal's partition in 1911 was only seemingly a triumph for Indian nationalism. It had been dealt a fatal blow by the introduction of separate electorates which ensured that only the most fanatical and vociferous among Muslims could get elected.

Despite the grant of separate electorates, Muslims felt agitated over the Khilafat issue. In India, as in several other countries, Muslims regarded the ruler of Turkey as their Khalifa or guardian. Anti-British feeling ran high when World War I broke out with Britain and Turkey ranged on opposite sides. An attack on Turkey by Greek troops in 1919 created bitter resentment. Gandhi, who had returned from South Africa and assumed the leadership of Indian National Congress, saw in the anti-British mood of Indian Muslims an opportunity to draw them into the freedom movement from which most of them had kept aloof. He began to placate Muslim sentiment and went so far on this course that it came to be described as Muslim appeasement.

Gandhi was initially opposed to a proposal by Muslims to boycott British goods as part of the Khilafat programme. He said at a Khilafat conference at Delhi on 24th November 1919 attended by both Muslim and Hindu leaders: "The Mussalmans have resolved that if the Government fail to secure them the fulfilment of their righteous demand, then they will cease to lend Government co-operation. But they have also adopted a step which looks ridiculous. They have decided to observe a progressive boycott of British goods in the event apprehended. We must have regard for the opinion of the world. We must enlist the sympathy of the world, and I therefore respectfully request you to forego boycott."

However, when leaders of the Indian Muslim community persisted in the demand for boycott, Gandhi reversed his attitude. He drew up in January 1921 an eleven-point programme of non-cooperation which included boycott of foreign goods. Bonfires of foreign cloth were made in Bombay city and elsewhere.

The next step in Gandhi's bending before Muslim pressure was his abandonment of Ahimsa, so far as Muslims were concerned. Moving the main resolution at a Khilafat meeting in Bombay on 19th March 1920, Gandhi who wanted Hindus to support the Muslims in their agitation, said: "The resolution commits the joint movement to a policy of non-violence in the course of the struggle. But Muslims have a special Koranic obligation in which Hindus may or may not join. They, therefore, reserve to themselves the right, in the event of failure of non-co-operation-cum-non-violence, in order to enforce justice, to resort to all such methods as may be enjoined in the Islamic scriptures." (D.G. Tendulkar's *Mahatma*, Vol. I, p. 346) Gandhi thus exempted Muslims from

Ahimsa, though, was an article of faith for himself which, he insisted, should be adhered to by this Hindu followers.

Of the many subsequent instances of Gandhi endorsing the demands of separatist Muslim leaders, I shall cite two. When objection was raised to the singing of "Vande Mataram", a song hailing Mother India, Gandhi advised that it should not be sung if there was objection from a single member (read Muslim) in a mixed gathering. The separation of the Muslim-majority district of Sind from Bombay Presidency was another Muslim demand which Gandhi endorsed. Sind became a separate Province under the Government of India Act of 1935. The March 1940 resolution came as a shock to Gandhi, against the background of his numerous expressions of goodwill for Muslims and the concessions made by him to Muslim sentiment. As recently as in 1939, the year before the Pakistan resolution, Gandhi told the Muslims of Rajkot, a princely State, that "if they wanted separate electorates in Rajkot with reservation of seats, I would see to it that they get them." This was in the context of the Hindu ruler of that principality citing alleged fears of the Muslim minority inducing them to stall the popular demand for self-government.

However, once Jinnah crossed the Rubicon and set out to vivisect India, Gandhi was unsparingly frank in rebutting the Muslim League's two-nation theory. He said to Louis Ficher when the American journalist interviewed him during June 1942: "Every Muslim will have a Hindu name if he goes back far enough in his family history." Jinnah himself had a recent Hindu ancestor named Jinabhai.

On one occasion Gandhi referred to the case of his eldest son Hiralal. He had worked closely with his father during the Satyagraha years in South Africa and earned the title of Junior Gandhi. But he increasingly resented what he saw as Gandhi's tyrannical behaviour, and became a Muslim as an expression of his revolt. Though the Arya Samaj reclaimed Hiralal for Hinduism after some time, he had become an alcoholic. In the context of the Muslim League's demand for the establishment of Muslim homelands, Gandhi asked sarcastically what was his son's homeland when he became a Muslim: his native Porbandar in Gujarat, or Punjab?

After the failure of the Quit India movement which Gandhi launched in August 1942 despite the reservations of some colleagues, he sought and secured the opportunity of talks with M.A. Jinnah, president of the Muslim League. During September 1944, Gandhi drove up fourteen times to the residence of Jinnah on Malabar Hill in Bombay, with never a return visit by the Qaid-e-Azam, a title denoting supreme leadership of Indian Muslims. In the course of the correspondence which was conducted along with the talks, Gandhi says in a letter of 15th September: "I find no parallel in history for a body of converts and their descendants claiming to be a nation apart from the parent stock. If India was one nation before the advent of Islam, it must remain one in spite of the change of faith of a very large body of her children." In the course of the same letter, he who had supported the pan-Islamic cause of Khilafat now asks Jinnah, in all innocence, "Is the goal of Pakistan pan-Islam?

With his fourteen calls on Jinnah, Gandhi unwittingly elevated him in the esteem of the general public and of Muslims in particular, and downgraded Maulana Azad, the Congress president, whom Jinnah derided as a 'showboy' of the Congress. This doubtless contributed to the outcome of the elections held in 1945 to the Central Legislative Assembly, in which the Muslim League won every Muslim seat. In the elections during 1945-46 to the provincial legislatures, the Muslim League won the majority of the Muslim seats in every Province except the North-West Frontier.

Jinnah dealt the final blow by calling for 'direct action' on 16th August 1946 to enforce the demand for Partition. In Calcutta—Bengal was then under a Muslim League government—Muslim mobs indulged in an orgy of murder and loot of Hindus and their property provoking retaliation by the city's Hindus. Communal riots spread from Calcutta to East Bengal and from there to Bihar and Punjab. Direct Action Day was a Friday, special day of prayer for Muslims, and Friday has continued in post-Partition India to be the day most frequent in outbreaks of arson by Muslims, pouring out of mosques after hearing inflammatory sermons. Pakistan became an accomplished fact a year after the Direct Action.

Borderless Religions, Semitic and Marxist

The root cause of this historic tragedy is neither the conferment of separate electorates on Indian Muslims by the British rulers, nor Gandhi's misconveyed though well-intentioned support to Khilafat. The cause is the nature of Islam, youngest and least reformed of the three Semitic monotheist religions. Zionism is the oldest.

The word 'zealot', to denote an extreme partisan or fanatic, is derived from the name of a Jewish sect which aimed at world Jewish theocracy. Its members resisted the Romans till 70 CE. Thanks to the vicissitudes of history the Jews became victims of persecution by Christians, and the young State of Israel is struggling to exist amidst hostile Muslim countries. Zionism has matured and mellowed sufficiently for the Chief Rabbi, Yona Metzger, to attend an inter-religious conference in Delhi in February 2007 in which participants included Hindu, Muslim and Sikh religious leaders. The Chief Rabbi said that Jews had lived in India for 2,000 years and have never been discriminated against: "This is something unparalleled in history." The

Jewish and Hindu delegations affirmed in a joint statement: "Neither seeks to proselytise, nor undermine or replace in any way the religious identity of other faith communities. They expect other faith communities to respect their religious identities." (Report in *Organiser*, February 18, 2007)

There is much in its history that Christianity has to live down: the expeditions known as the Crusades to recover Jerusalem from Muslims, which the C.O.D. describes as "war instigated by the Church for alleged religious ends"; the cruel Inquisition conducted by Catholic missionaries in Goa when it was under Portuguese rule; and the complicity of the Church in European colonialism in Asia and Africa and in the slave trade. In 1727 the Bishop of London addressed a letter to the slave-owners in the southern colonies of America: "Christianity and the embracing of the gospel does not make the least alteration in civil property or in any of the duties which belong to civil relations...as to their outward condition, whatsoever that was before, whether bond or free, their being baptised and becoming Christians makes no manner of change in them."

The Reformation which saw the rise of national churches independent of Rome, had a liberalising effect. Even during the colonial period, some of the reformed churches threw up such admirable personalities as Charles F. Andrews, a friend and co-worker of Gandhi's who was affectionately described by Indians, after his initials, as Christ's Faithful Apostle. But the Catholic Church, which commands the allegiance of the great majority of Christians the world over, continues to be committed to evangelism. The former Pope (John Paul

II), on a visit to India in November 1999, called for a harvesting of souls in Asia during the third millennium even as Christianity had earlier been 'planted', as he put it, in Europe and America.

In the case of Islam there has been little change from the time of its inception and its early growth through conquest. Islam has had nothing comparable to the Reformation in the West, or to the humane influences which reformed Brahminism in India. Brahminism had divided people into Brahmins and non-Brahmins, and the latter in turn into grades of inequality, much as Islam was later to divide mankind into believers and Kafirs. Whereas in India there were liberalising influences which transformed Brahminism into Hinduism, Islam has had no counterparts of India's Upanishadic thinkers, the Jain and Buddhist reformers or the Bhakti movement, except for Sufism.

Though Sufism was not widespread in India, it produced an outstanding personality, Dara Shikoh, through whose translation the Upanishads became known to the West. Dara was one of the four sons of emperor Shah Jahan, on whose failing ill in September 1657 a war of succession broke out. Aurangzeb, who combined religious fanaticism with ruthlessness in the pursuit of power, emerged the victor. Crowning himself emperor in Delhi in 1658, he had his elder brother Dara executed the following year after getting him condemned by the Mullahs as an apostate for deviating from the Islamic faith.

Dara was indeed guilty of deviation if Islamic faith means Islam. Dara was a friend of the Sufi sage Sarmad who said of himself that he had passed from Jewish faith into Islam and, on coming to India, "wandered into the garden of Sri Rama and Laxman." Dara, an Indian by birth and a Muslim by upbringing, took a respectful interest in the religious thought of the Hindus. He found that Advaita or non-duality was manifest from "their heavenly books which are the Rig Veda, the Yajur Veda, the Sama Veda and the Atharva Veda. And it can also be ascertained from the holy Koran that there is no nation without a prophet and without a revealed scripture. The summum bonum of the four books are called the Upanishads. Dara says further in the course of the preface to his translation into Persian of a selection of Upanisadic verses, referring to himself in the third person: "He (Dara) obtained from these the essence of the most ancient of all heavenly books in point of time. Happy is he who shall study and comprehend this translation entitled Sirr-C-Akbar (The Great Secret), knowing it to be a translation of the words of God." It was from a Latin and subsequently French translation of Dara Shikoh's Persian rendering that the West came to know of the Upanishads for the first time.

K.R. Qanungo, biographer of Dara Shikoh, has said: "Anyone who intends to take up the solution of the problem of religious peace in India must begin the work where Dara had left it, and proceed on the path chalked out by that prince." But, to India's misfortune, neither Gandhi nor Nehru was aware of Dara Shikoh and his significant contribution. This is surprising since both were close friends of Maulana Azad, whose appraisal of Dara Shikoh is a classic of liberal religious thought and of literary expression. Azad wrote in 1910 an essay on Sarmad Shaheed (martyr) in the course of which he says: "During the last days of Emperor Shah Jahan, Dara

Shikoh was heir-apparent. A man of Sufi temperament, he was unique among Mughal princes. It is a blot on historical veracity that the pen which recorded the history of the Mughal period was always held by Prince Dara Shikoh's enemies. Dara's writings indicate that the author was a man of excellent taste. The overwhelming proof of his taste is that in pursuing his goal he lost the distinction between the temple and the mosque. The humility with which he met the Muslim divines was matched by the devotion with which he bowed his head before the Hindu saints and sadhus. Who can deny the purity this principle? Because, in this exalted state of mind, if one can still distinguish between Kufr and Islam, then what is the difference between blindness and vision? The moth should seek the flame. If it is desirous of the lamp which is lit only in the mosque, its desire for self-immolation is not complete."

Abul Kalam Azad was barely 21 when he wrote this magnificent essay. Within a decade, he was overtaken by Pan-Islamist fervour during the Khilafat movement, and suffered a spiritual counterpart of the hardening of arteries. Like the English poet Wordsworth who was in his youth a mystic and a worshipper of nature but, over the years turned into an orthodox Christian, Maulana Azad became a conventional Muslim though he continued to be a nationalist. The essay on Sarmad remained a literary masterpiece; its theme did not permeate his later speeches and writings.

Closer to our times lived another Indian humanist who deserves to be known more widely than he is. M. Asaf Ali (1898–1953) knew and was proud of India's pre-Islamic cultural heritage. His interest in the Mahabharata and the ancient schools of Indian philosophy was so deep that his friends would refer to him banteringly as 'Pandit' Asaf Ali.

Innate in him, as in Gandhi, was the Rigvedic type of natural religion: "At odd moments; when I feel one with the visible and invisible reality of the universe, I am convinced that behind, throughout and ahead of all is a living power, eternal and infinite. For lack of a better expression I call it God." Asaf Ali translated into Urdu a play by Aeschylus, Greek playwright of the fifth century BCE, entitled 'The Persians', from an English version. This play, like the Mahabharata, brings out the tragedy and futility of war, the vast empathy of Aeschylus embracing the foe in war as well as the compatriot. This was doubtless the reason why Asaf Ali chose it for translation.

Asaf Ali also wrote stories for the young, some of which he sent by post to his wife Aruna when both of them were in different jails at Lahore in 1931. One of these stories tells of a gardener who is asked by his wife who is working alongside him: "Why must we toil to produce these roses? Why don't roses grow from the marble floor of palaces?" The gardener replies: "Kings may tamper with mountains and make them yield porphyrie and marble, and precious stones, but they cannot tamper with the soil which alone yields sweet-scented flowers; the creator of earth dreams in flowers only."

How little was the influence of Sufism and of nationalist Muslims with a humane outlook like Maulana Azad and Asaf Ali was shown by developments since 1937, when elections were held in all the provinces under the government of India Act of 1935 which granted provincial autonomy. The Congress swept all the General (predominantly Hindu) seats. M.A. Jinnah, who had assumed leadership of the Muslim League, wanted that coalition governments including the League should be formed in each province, even where the League's presence in the legislature was negligible. When the Congress did not agree, Jinnah declared: "Muslims can expect neither justice nor fair play under Congress governments." The Muslim League was quick to fill the political vacuum created by the resignation of the Congress Ministries in eleven provinces in 1939 in protest against India being dragged into World War II without consultation. The Pakistan resolution followed quickly in 1940, and the realisation of the demand followed in 1947. There was a non-Muslim political party which supported the demand for partition: the Communist Party of India.

In a book on the implications of Pakistan, published in 1940, B.R. Ambedkar who was a greater political realist than both Gandhi and Nehru, urged that in the event of partition, there should be an orderly transfer of population as a logical corollary to Jinnah's two-nation theory. If this suggestion needed any precedent in its favour, it was there in the Civilian Internees' Camp established during World War II by the British authorities at Dehra Dun for German and Italians resident in India at the outbreak of the war. It was felt that their sympathies would be with the countries of their origin, and they might therefore render help to the Axis Powers unless they were immobilised.

Such was the powerful hold of the idea of Pakistan on the minds of Indian Muslims that, except in the North

West Frontier, they voted overwhelmingly for the Muslim League in the provincial elections held in 1946. It is remarkable that the Muslim League managed to get only a majority of Muslim-reserved seats in the Muslim-majority provinces of Punjab and Bengal, but made a clean sweep of all the Muslim seats in certain Muslim-minority provinces: Bombay, Madras and Orissa. These provinces could not possibly become part of Pakistan. If the Muslim voters of Madras who spoke Telugu, Tamil or Malayalam thought they might somehow get to Pakistan, what would they do in the promised land where none of these languages was prevalent? Similarly with the Marathi and Gujarati speaking Muslims of Bombay province, and the Oriya speaking Muslims. That they all voted for the Muslim League and for Partition showed the triumph of the Islamist mind over ethnic and social reality.

The tragedy of the Partition holocaust in Bengal, Bihar and Punjab might have been avoided if the British rulers as well as the Congress had insisted that Jinnah should agree to a transfer of population in terms of his own two-nation theory. It would have made India, though territorially diminished, not only politically free but free of the Hindu-Muslim problem which was a consequence of the Islamic invasions and which persists to this day.

This survey of the major monotheist religions will be incomplete without a reference to Communism, also called Marxism. Though godless in ideology, it too proudly calls itself 'borderless'. Strangers to territorial nationalism, and free from territorial attachment to India as motherland, Indian Communists supported the

British rulers during World War II after Hitler's attack on Russia in June 1941. This event, according to them transformed what had till then been an imperialist war into a people's war. Since Britain and their ideological fatherland were now allies, they turned against the Congress which wanted Britain to quit India. The Muslim League from the beginning supported Britain's war effort in India. Muslim separatists and Communists were now on the same side. Communists extended support to the League's demand for Muslim homelands, and rationalised it as follows (in the words of B.T. Ranadive): "What is the progressive demand of the Pakistan demand? The application of the principle of self-determination to certain nationalities in India. Muslims in certain areas do form a distinct nationality bound together by common culture, history and tradition. In consonance with the demands of justice and fair play, they must have the complete liberty to build their own life, a liberty sanctioned by the right to form a separate State if and when chosen. Unification of India cannot be built except on this basis of complete freedom of nationalities to secede." A consequence of this for me was my resignation from the CPI. I had joined the party early in 1944, at the age of seventeen while studying at Presidency College in Madras, much impressed by the Communists' humanitarian work during the Bengal famine. As I told my comrades of the college party cell, while surrendering the party card, I could not canvass with others a party line which did not convince me.

In the elections held to the legislatures after the war, Communists supported Muslim League candidates in the Muslim constituencies and contributed to the League's sweeping victory. Communists thus bear a share of a responsibility for the division of India amid bloodshed and arson in a virtual Hindu-Muslim civil war across northern India following the 'direct action' called by Jinnah in August 1946.

Just as Christianity and Islam became an excuse and cover for colonial conquest, Communism at the close of World War II grew into an empire. Soviet forces did not withdraw from the countries of Eastern Europe which they liberated from German occupation. They crushed a nationalist uprising in Hungary in 1956, and invaded Czechoslovakia in 1968. Tension grew between the U.S.A. and Soviet Russia. The Communist faithful throughout the world conducted a strident 'peace' campaign during the years that Soviet Russia lacked nuclear weaponry to match that of the Americans. The Cold War between the big Two ended when following the collapse of its state-run economy, the Soviet Union (born in 1917) broke up in 1991.

Communist China, born in 1949 with Mao Tse-tung heading it, had meanwhile given up statist economics in favour of a market economy. But Mao's successors did not give up their political dictatorship. Members of India's two major Communist parties—CPI and CPI (M) have by now become gentlemen communists, but the fate of the Russian and Chinese experiments in Communism has not deterred Naxalites and Maoists from their course of insurrection entailing revolutionary dacoity and the killing of policemen and suspected informers. The history of fanatical creeds, whether theist or atheist, is a study in the deadly mix of initial idealism and ruthless pursuit of power.

Islamist Mind Over Ethnic Matter

In a country where Islam has been transplanted, the nature of the initial interaction has depended on its ethnic background, history and culture. An example is Indonesia, where Hindu cultural influence was widespread before the coming of Islam. I recall two anecdotes narrated by an elder friend, G. Parthasarathi who was India's ambassador to Indonesia during 1957–58. When he presented his credentials, President Soekarno looked thoughtfully at the name and remarked: "Partha is Arjuna, and Sarathi is charioteer. So you are really Krishna!" The very name of Indonesia's first President is revealing. Soekarno is a variant of "Sukarna". The name was coined by his father who admired the Mahabharata and was attracted by the personality of Karna, the generous-souled warrior. But he was not happy that Karna should have ranged himself on the side of the unrighteous Kauravas. Wanting his son to be a 'good Karna' he named him Sukarna.

The other anecdote concerns Mohammad Hatta. As Vice President of Indonesia he was due to visit India, and the ambassador met him to discuss the proposed itinerary. Included in the programme was a meeting with some Indian Maulvis. Hatta looked puzzled. After Parthasarathi explained that the term referred to Muslim divines, he exclaimed 'Oh! You mean Maha Gurus! Yes, yes.' But the vogue of India's epics, in drama and ballet, has declined in Indonesia following the inflow of Islamic petro-dollars from West Asia, especially Saudi Arabia, since the 1970s.

Malaysia is another country where, after conversion, Islam sat lightly on the Malay inhabitants (55%) who lived amicably with the Chinese (25%), Buddhists and Christians and Indians (15%, mostly Hindus). But in Malaysia too, following the inflow of petro-dollars, Islamism has been on the rise. The destruction of several Hindu temples, mainly in 2006, has come to light recently.

In India itself, another country where Islam was a transplant, Islam sat lightly on converted Hindus for very long, till the beginning of the twentieth century when politics intervened. Muslim separatism was fostered by British colonial officials in pursuit of their policy of divide-and-rule, and by some ambitious Indian Muslim leaders who wanted a vote bank for themselves in separate Muslim electorates.

The early Census reports bear witness to the fact that till the end of the 19th century the caste of their Hindu origin was more real to the converts than the newly acquired religion. E.A. Gait of the Indian Civil Service, a Fellow of the royal Statistical Society, supervised the 1911 Census which revealed a total of 66.6 million Muslims in the country (more than 20%). His Report, published in 1913 by the Superintendent of Government Printing at Calcutta, quotes from time to time the observations of district officers. It says: "Many descendants of persons 'converted' to Islam are far from being genuine Muhammadans, though they have been classed as such in the Census. Of these, the Malkanas of the country around Agra furnish a striking instance. 'These' says Mr. Gait, 'were converted Hindus of various castes belonging to Agra and the adjoining districts, chiefly Muttra, Etah and Mainpuri. They are of Rajput, Jat and Bania descent. They are reluctant to describe themselves as Musalmans, and generally give their caste name. Their names are Hindu; they mostly worship in Hindu temples; they use the salutation, 'Raam, Raam';

they inter-marry amongst themselves only. On the other hand, they sometimes frequent a mosque, practice circumcision, and bury their dead; they will eat with Muhammadans if they are particular friends; they prefer to be addressed as Mian Thakur. They admit that they are neither Hindus nor Muhammadans, but a mixture of both. Of late, some of them have definitely abjured Islam."

The Bombay Superintendent classes a certain caste, numbering some 35,000, as Hindu–Muhammadans, "adding a new category to the religious terminology. The boundary line between Hindus on the one hand and Sikhs (from 'Sewak') and Jains on the other is even more indeterminate: 44,000 returned their religion as Sikh Hindus."

According to the Report, of 12 million Muslims in Punjab, 10 million gave caste identification, indicating that they were originally Hindus. That a thin dividing line which separated Hindus and Muslims till the dawn of the 20th century became within a few decades an insurmountable wall shows how a monotheist religion, in the hands of fanatics, can become a weapon of mass destruction. This was to be demonstrated again in 2002 in widely separated parts of the world. In New York, Jehadis hijacked two aeroplanes and rammed them into the twin towers of the World Trade Centre, causing large-scale loss of life and property. In the Indonesian island of Bali, many holidaymakers and others of different nationalities, were killed in an Islamic terror attack. Such has been the bitter harvest of a fanatical 'borderless' religion aiming at world hegemony.

British Rule, Nationalism and Separatism

British traders and administrators made a creeping conquest of India, deploying English forces in support of one local ruler against another. Not being military missionaries like the Muslim invaders, they were not keen to invite Christian missionaries to come over. But they did come, and this led to an augmentation of the population of Indian Christians, of whom there were already a large number in the native States of Travancore and Cochin, belonging to the old Syrian Church of a period much before the East India Company. The 1911 Census Report placed the total of Christians at 3.9 million, or 1.2 per cent of the population. Of these, 3.6 million were Indian Christians and the rest Europeans nearly 200,000 and Anglo-Indians (above 100,000), the latter born mainly of Indian mothers. The increase in Indian Christians was three-fold since 1872, and had doubled (at an accelerated rate) since 1881.

There are some parallels with the earlier conversions to Islam during Muslim rule. "Missionaries", the Report says, "find it easier to convert depressed castes of Madras and Punjab, and hill tribes of Chota Nagpur and Assam than to convert high caste Hindus or Muslims." Other sources for conversion included the Mahars of Central Provinces and Berar. Brahminism with its Chatur Varna social gradation thus made its contribution of recruits to "Christianity, as earlier to Islam. There is also acknowledgement of the role of inducement in conversions: "In Kaira, many converted during famine returned to their ancestral beliefs."

E.A. Gait, who supervised the 1911 Census, says in the Report: "Many Hindus send their children to mission schools and colleges. In this way Christian thought influences large numbers who remain Hindus, and Christian ideals and standards are everywhere gaining vogue. The European reader of Indian newspapers is often astonished at the writers' familiarity with the Bible."

The Brahmo Samaj founded by Rammohun Roy was suffused with Christianity. Gandhi employed Biblical language and imagery freely, as in the course of his address on economic and moral progress at the Muir College Economic Society, Allahabad, on 22nd September 1916. He recalled Christ's injunction, "Take no thought for the morrow." Gandhi went on to cite from Mark: "Go thy way, sell whatever thou hast, and give to the poor." Again, from Luke: "Ye cannot serve God and Mammon."

The English language has attracted vastly more converts—before and after India's independence—than the Christian religion has been able to attract. However, the intrusive evangelism of some missionaries from sundry parts of the Christian world has been a source of nuisance and annoyance.

It was not only the gospels that influenced Gandhi. There is a list of books read by him, and commended by him to the reader, attached to *Hind Swaraj*, a seminal work in which he denounces the evils of industrialism and presents his own alternative of decentralised production, based on local resources of material and labour and designed to meet local needs. The list includes a book by Henry David Thoreau that inspired Gandhi's strategy of non-violent non-cooperation to end foreign rule in India. In the essay, 'On the duty of disobedience' Thoreau writes: "When the subject has refused his allegiance, and the officer has resigned his office, then the revolution is accomplished." Thoreau also wrote a book on Walden Pond which in its intimate love of nature calls the Rigvedic poems to mind and is rather like Gandhi's writing on 'tree worship' and sleeping under the stars.

Like Rammohun Roy who headed India's re-awakening in the modern period, the leaders of the freedom movement were proficient in English: Bal Gangadhar Tilak, Lala Lajpat Rai, Aurobindo Ghose, Gandhi and Nehru. They spoke to the middle class all over India which was taking increasingly to English education. English literature with its many patriotic poems, the example of the American war of independence, and the British leaders' avowal of advance towards self-government as the goal were factors which fostered the growth of national feeling. Sanskrit had been a pan-Indian language from ancient times. But it was confined to a small Brahmin elite. Persian, though it was the language of the administration during Muslim rule, did not become widely diffused. In contrast, English became a common second language for educated Indians who spoke different mother tongues. The growth of transport and communications was another factor which promoted the consciousness of India as one country.

Division: After Religion, Caste

Partition of Bengal at the dawn of the twentieth century was deliberately designed by the British rulers to divide the Muslims from the Hindus of the province. Curzon, the Viceroy, while commending his partition scheme reminded Muslims that they had been the ruling race in the country, and would now get, in eastern Bengal, a territory of their own where they could prosper. Curzon was succeeded by Minto, who received a stage-managed Muslim delegation which asked for separate electorates so that they could elect their own true representatives to legislatures throughout the country. Minto's secretary informed Lady Minto, in a note which he wrote the same evening, that they had succeeded in preventing a part of India's population from joining the ranks of the 'seditious opposition'.

In contrast to the deliberate creation of a rift between the Hindu and Muslim communities, the promotion of caste differences within the Hindu community, which followed, was in the nature of encouragement rather than incitement. Conversions to Islam following the Muslim invasions—and subsequently to Christianity during British rule—were from the lowest castes of the Sudra 'Varna'. This was the fourth and despised group in the Brahminist scheme of Chatur Varna, set out in the Purusha Sukta, which is a Brahminist hymn smuggled into the last book of Rigveda.

The converts to Islam were totally lost to the Hindu community, and it is the descendants of these converts who form the bulk of the population of present-day Pakistan and Bangladesh. Most of the Sudras—i.e. those ranking below Brahmins, Kshatriyas and Vaisyas—were not converted to Islam or Christianity but they remained disaffected because of their low place in the social and economic scale.

The 'untouchables' or Depressed Classes (Gandhi called them Harijan or children of God) were not a fifth caste, but belonged to the lowest among the Sudra castes. The former untouchables were listed in a Schedule to the Constitution of free India which came into force in 1950, and are therefore known as the Schedules Castes. The foremost political leader of the Depressed Classes was B.R. Ambedkar, who was a Mahar, an untouchable caste of Maharashtra. He wanted not merely that there should be a quota of seats in the legislature reserved for the Depressed Classes, but that only the Depressed Classes should vote for one or other of the candidates contesting these reserved seats. In other words, he wanted a separate electorate of Depressed Classes, on the lines of the separate electorates which had been created in the case of Muslims. This would have separated the Depressed Classes from the main body of Hindus, just as Muslims already stood separated. When, in 1932, the British government awarded separate electorates for Depressed Classes, Gandhi went on an indefinite fast in protest. Ambedkar was constrained, in order to save Gandhi's life, to agree to a compromise formula. Under this formula, voting would be by all the electors in a reserved constituency but the candidates would have to be from a panel of names approved by the Depressed Classes. This was meant to remove the fear that a candidate from a Depressed Class liable to be controlled by others might get elected.

In the early decades of the 20th century in Madras Presidency, Brahmins were at the forefront in the national movement led by the congress. They also occupied high positions in professions like law and medicine. This led to a movement for the educational and social advancement of non-Brahmins, the term covering the spectrum of castes from Kshatriya to Sudras other than the Depressed Classes. Some leaders of this movement like P. Tyagaraya Chetty opposed Annie Besant's demand for Home Rule. In 1925, E.V. Ramaswami Naicker said that the Brahmin question should be settled during British supremacy, otherwise they would have to suffer under 'Brahminocracy'. Later he went so far as to say that Tamil Nadu should secede from India. On the non-Brahmin movement, which took the shape of the Justice Party, *The Hindu* commented in April 1925 when Tyagaraya Chetty passed away: "If separatism was elevated to a principle of political action, it was done because the accumulated grievances of centuries had rendered it inevitable." (*A Hundred Years of The Hindu* by R. Parthasarathy, p. 338) Such were the separatist consequences of the Brahminism with its caste hierarchy which supplanted the humane ethos of mutualism upheld by the rigvedic poet-thinkers.

Till the Government of India Act of 1935 provided substantial provincial autonomy, the governments in the provinces functioned under a system of diarchy, exercising power in respect of only some subjects; the legislatures were elected on a highly restricted franchise. It was during this period—1921 to 1937—that the Justice Party introduced the reservation of a certain number of seats in the legislature for non-Brahmins. It also reserved a percentage of posts in public services, and seats in colleges for specified backward castes. This was the beginning of a policy of caste-based positive discrimination.

Birds of a feather flock together. E.V. Ramaswamy Naicker wrote to M.A. Jinnah on the eve of the Gandhi–

Jinnah talks in 1944, reminded him "about our discussions relating to Pakistan and Dravidastan while we were at Madras and Delhi, and your assurance that you would plead for both questions as one." Jinnah in his reply said he had noticed that Naicker and his colleagues had been 'indecisive': "If the people of your province really desire Dravidastan, then it is for them to assert themselves ... You will find me supporting any just and fair claim of any section of the people of India and particularly the non-Brahmins of India."

This correspondence was released following the expulsion of Ramaswami Naicker by the Justice Party for launching for Dravida Kazhagam, an organisation whose aims diverged from its own.

Postscript

At the conclusion of this self-chosen task, I feel all over again the sense of fulfilment that my compilation of an album of the music of Sripada Pinakapani gave me seven years ago. My discovery of that singer was in the early 1960s. Over the following decades I made many recordings of his unaccompanied singing for my own listening. It was while 'documenting' him in 1993 for the Sangeet Natak Akademi that the idea struck me of bringing out a selection of his music from my collection. The dream was realised in December 1999.

It was also in the early 1960s that I made my first acquaintance with some poems from the Rigveda, through *Sources of Indian Tradition* (Columbia University Press, 1963.). This stimulated the study of a number of other selections from, and eventually a full translation of the Rigveda, as well as related books on India's religion and philosophy. The outcome is the presentation, in these pages, of the lovely face of the pristine Rigveda, with its message of a caring and sharing society united for self-defence.

Pinakapani's music was for me an experience of transcendence through art. Exploration of the Rigveda has given me the joy of an enlarged and deepened perception of the world and of human life. The two discoveries make me feel that perhaps mine has been 'a life not altogether wasted'.

Bibliography

An Advance History of India, R.C. Majumdar, Macmillan, 1950.

Ancient Indian Literature - An Anthology, G. Kashihar, Sahitya Academy, 2000.

Anthology of Ancient Indian Literature, Sahitya Academy, 2008.

Anthology in Chawaka Lokayata Edited by D.P. Chattopadhayaya and M.K. Gangopadhyaya, Indian Council of Philosophic Research, 1990.

A source book on Indian Philosophy-Dr. S. Radhakrishnan, Princeton, 1957.

Bhagavad Gita-Kisari Mohan Ganguli Munshiram Monoharlal, 1981.

Hindu Samskara-a socio-religious study of Hindu Sacraments-Raj Bali Pandey, Vikram Publications, Banaras.

Hinduism-Essence and Consequence, Arun Shourie.

Indian Heritage - Dr. V. Raghavan, 1958.

Kaundunja Smriti - Gopal Publications Hyderabad 2004.

Mahetone -D.G. Tendulkar.

Memories-Asaf Ali-Ajanta Publications, 1995.

Mohenjodaro and the Indus Civilization, Sir John Marshall.

Myths and Legends of India - J.M. Macfie, Rupa, New Delhi.

One Vedic Reader A. Macdonnell 1917 Reprinted by Motilal Banarsidass 1992.

Rigveda Samhita Translated by Max Mullar Oxford University Press, 1890.

Rig Vedic Study M. Sundarraj, Madras, 1994.

Seers and Thinkers- A.C. Bose, Cultural leaders of India Series: Publications Division.

Sources of Indian Tradition - R.N. Dandekar-Columbia University Press 1963, Reprinted by Motilal Banarsidass.

Sources of Indian Tradition - A.L. Bashan.

The Hymns of the Rig Veda - R.T.H. Griffith, Reprinted by Motilal Banarsidass, 1896.

The Ramayana of Valmiki-Vikas.

The Third Morality Gerald Heard Cassell, 1933.

The Vedic Experience-Darhan Longman and Jodd, London, 1977.

Vedic People; their History and Geography, Rajesh Kochar, Orient Longman, 2000.

Who were the Sudras-Dr. B.R. Ambedkar, Thacher, 1946.

Index

D

E

N

O

P

R